The Free Offer And The Call Of The Gospel

The Free Offer

and the Call of the Gospel

George M. Ella

Go *publications*

The Free Offer

Go Publications

Gibb Hill Farm, Ponsonby, Cumbria, CA20 1BX, ENGLAND

© Go Publications 2017
First Published 2001
This edition 2017

ISBN 978-1-908475-05-3

Printed and bound in Great Britain by Lightning Source

Table Of Contents

The Free Offer

Introduction

The Free Offer is a key part of modern evangelical preaching. It is used to describe a popular approach to evangelism and to explain an imagined lack of consistency between the Biblical doctrine of sovereign grace and the church's obligation to preach the gospel to every creature.

The 'free offer' preacher presumes to invite all sinners to believe on the Lord Jesus Christ, promising them salvation if they do. This he does even if he holds that Christ's atonement was neither made for all, nor intended for all who hear the gospel message.

The following study demonstrates that the modern free offer contradicts free grace. Consequently, free offer evangelism is unbiblical and another gospel. How, for example, can we reconcile God's purpose to save only some, redeem only some, freely and unconditionally bestow the gift of faith on only some, with a genuine free offer to *all* to believe and be saved?

The Free Offer

Terms such as 'sincere' and 'well-meant' are sometimes applied to the free offer to indicate that the salvation on offer is real and genuine. But we reply that except salvation is *actually accomplished* by Jesus Christ, it is merely notional and any 'offer' is disingenuous. Indeed, the free offer is a mockery of the spiritual inability of the reprobate or non-elect.

The free offer is works mixed with grace. It imposes a duty on the sinner to believe savingly in Christ even though the gift of faith is never granted.

Let it be noted in all studies of this subject that advocates of the free offer, whether they admit it or not, are preaching their free, sincere and well meant offers *on God's behalf.* That is to say, the teaching assumes, as will be shown in the pages that follow, that it is not the preacher with his limited knowledge, but the all-knowing, eternal God who freely, sincerely, and genuinely offers salvation to all mankind. This is in spite of the Father's eternal purpose to save only the elect, the substitutionary nature of Christ's atoning work and the distinguishing, effectual call of the Holy Spirit.

There are only two courses open to all free offer preachers. Either, they must preach a mongrel gospel of works and duty where the sinner is urged to commit to a Saviour who is ill-defined and a way of salvation that is necessarily vague—such preachers generally ignore anything to do with God's electing decrees, the Divine source of repentance and faith, the purposely limited extent of the atonement and the necessity of Holy Spirit regeneration. Or else, they must try to establish an alternative doctrinal basis, other than the shed blood of Jesus Christ, upon which to offer salvation to all,

In the pages that follow Dr Ella carefully unpicks and explains the history of the free offer controversy. He points to early attempts by Hugo Grotius on the Continent, Andrew Fuller in England and the New Divinity School in America, to establish a basis, outside of the atonement, for belief-obligation or duty faith by the sinner, still in his natural state. He goes on to show how these early efforts have been adapted and enlarged upon by many modern 'Reformed' teachers.

This study will prove invaluable to those who are troubled by a lack of doctrinal clarity in modern evangelical and evangelistic preaching and the unhealthy emphasis on man and man's will that is creeping unawares even into the most orthodox of circles.

The privilege of labouring in the Lord's harvest and evangelising the unconverted is amongst the highest blessings bestowed upon the Christian Church and one that we take very seriously. Therefore, it is essential that we know *who* we preach, *what* we preach, and *how* we preach the gospel properly to the unsaved. Or, as Paul succinctly puts it, 'We preach Christ crucified, unto the Jews a stumblingblock, and unto the Greeks foolishness; But unto them which are the called, both Jews and Greeks, Christ the power of God, and the wisdom of God' (1 Corinthians 1:23, 24).

Our reservations about free offer preaching must not inhibit our efforts to see the gospel freely proclaimed and widely disseminated. It does not restrict our desire to discover it, by God's grace, extensively received. Yet we must be careful that the gospel which is proclaimed is the whole gospel, the genuine article and the true message of salvation by grace through which repentance is granted and faith bestowed. We believe in a particular gospel promiscuously preached, and to that end wholeheartedly accept our divine obligations in the service of the Lord and King, our precious Saviour Jesus Christ.

It is my belief that the following pages will supply the open-minded reader with two important lessons. First, sound reasons for rejecting the 'free offer' method of evangelising. Second, solid scriptural principles by which our commission to preach the gospel of sovereign grace to every creature can properly be met.

Peter L. Meney

Dedicated to:

Those who search for gospel truth
upon old paths and in good ways

Jeremiah 6:16 Thus saith the LORD, Stand ye in the ways,
and see, and ask for the old paths, where *is* the good way,
and walk therein, and ye shall find rest for your souls. But
they said, We will not walk *therein.*

11

The Free Offer

The Free Offer
Dissected And Analysed

Atonement for all?

Preaching the gospel must take into consideration two major factors: the provisions of our holy God and the needs of sinful man. God's gospel provisions for sinful man are grounded in the atonement made by Jesus Christ. This atonement was worked out by Christ's human death as the sinner's substitute in His vicariously bearing the punishment of their sin and becoming their Saviour by granting them eternal life. The Christian gospel is thus nothing more and certainly nothing less than the good news that Jesus saves.

The big question is, however, what are the Father's exact provisions for salvation, and whom does the Son actually save? In much modern understanding of evangelism, i.e. the process of preaching the gospel which brings salvation, there is a certain predominant but highly questionable view.

The Free Offer

Evangelical Arminianism

We are told by some preachers that Christ's saving work, which they call God's provisions, must be balanced off by a display of human acceptance which they call human agency. For such would-be evangelists, man is left to accept or leave salvation as he wishes. He must either take the chance of everlasting life or lose it. By this scheme it is the preacher's job to tell everybody that Christ has atoned for their sins, but it is the sinner who must clinch the deal by accepting it. Thus, when the evangelist makes a gospel presentation to the sinner, telling him that salvation is there for the taking, he awaits an either-or response from those who hear him. The response is according to what the sinner thinks of the proposal, or how persuasive the evangelist himself is. Indeed, the early contenders for what has become known as the 'free offer' called their preaching 'moral suasion' or the art of persuading men to receive Christ as their Saviour. They thought that the right kind of moral man will accept the offer to his eternal benefit and the wrong kind will reject it to his eternal loss. This is called co-working with God. He has supplied the means for salvation which must be appropriated and applied by man as a free agent. Thus the function of the preacher is to present his argument so convincingly that the sinner will be persuaded to follow Christ.

The corollary of this partnership preaching: God has done His bit, now the sinner must do his: is that the saving work on the cross is seen as a universal action on the part of Christ who so loved every man that He atoned for all their sins. This atonement is thus there for all men everywhere. It was with this gospel in their heart that John and Charles Wesley could sing:

1. Father, whose everlasting love
Thy only Son for sinners gave,
Whose grace to *all* did freely move,
And sent him down *the world* to save:

2. Help us Thy mercy to extol,
Immense, unfathomed, unconfined;
To praise the Lamb who died for *all*,
The *general* Saviour of mankind.

3. Thy undistinguishing regard
Was cast on Adam's fallen race;
For all thou hast in Christ prepared
Sufficient, sovereign, saving grace.

4. The *world* he suffered to redeem;
For *all* he hath the atonement made;
For those who will not come to him
The ransom of his life was paid.

5. Why then, thou universal love,
Should any of thy grace despair?
To *all,* to *all,* thy bowels move,
But straightened in our own we are.

6. Arise, O God, maintain thy cause!
The fulness of the Gentiles call;
Lift up the standard of thy cross,
And *all* shall own thou diedst for all[1]

Here the way of the Wesleyan salvation is made clear. Christ died to save everyone, He is thus the general Saviour of all. This absolute and all-embracing salvation is, nevertheless, mitigated by saying that Christ has enough saving grace for all, though there are those who will not accept it. The aim of Christian preaching is thus to convince all, through claiming God's will in the matter, that Christ has died for all. The preacher's prayer is thus:

---

[1] Hymn 39, *Wesley Hymns and New Supplement.* The hymn bears an asterisk, indicating that it was not published during John Wesley's life and the title bears a 'W' which indicates that it is not known whether John or Charles wrote it.

O for a trumpet voice,
On *all the world* to call!
To bid their hearts rejoice
In Him who died for all;
For *all* my Lord was crucified,
For all, for *all* my Saviour died.[2]

Optimistic and all-embracing as this view of Christ's atonement is, there are obvious, puzzling factors in it. The term 'atonement' usually brings with it the meaning of sins covered, sins removed, sins forgiven and even sins remembered no more. This is because through atonement, sinners are reconciled to God. Nevertheless, the Wesleys tell us that though this atonement is wrought out for all, some do not take advantage of it. So, we are left with sins covered, sins removed, sins forgiven and sins remembered no more and sinners reconciled to God—but they will have nothing to do with it! God has done all but for those who spite God, He has done all in vain. Man's agency has stumped God's provisions! Man has shown his ability to thwart God and God must retreat!

Those who have knowledge of Wesleyan Arminianism and its teaching of free will in accepting or rejecting the gospel, might discard this teaching with the contempt it deserves if they have been tutored in a Reformed

---

[2] Ibid, from Let earth and heaven agree, Hymn 34, Charles Wesley.

The Free Offer

atmosphere which claims 'By grace are ye saved through faith; and that not of yourselves: it is the gift of God'.[3] Sadly, however, in recent years, there has been a turning away in the Reformed churches from the orthodox belief in a God who saves and secures a chosen people with His irresistible grace. Such preaching does not go down well in revival evangelism, our once 'Reformed' men now tell us. The result is that though originally John Wesley to them was a major heretic, now they are practically accepting his teaching. They find it friendlier to man and in agreement psychologically with man's view of himself as the one and only arbiter of his own life. It is here that many modern preachers, of even the Reformed side, prove themselves to be false prophets. We now find them teaching that God's saving purpose is not to secure and bestow salvation but to make salvation possible for all. These preachers feel that salvation must be available for everyone and thus boost up man's idea of his own ability. They teach that God's provisions are in vain unless man's agency accepts them. Leaving the doctrine of the atonement entirely out of the picture, they now emphasise in preaching that God desires the salvation of all sinners. This warrants the preacher to tell all that Christ loves all savingly. Consequently, sinners are now told, 'Christ desires and wants you so much that he has died for you'.

---

[3] Ephesians 2:8.

go *Topical*

Moderate Calvinism

This teaching, in its more modern development comes from the USA. The so-called New Divinity School of North America produced such popular evangelists as Joseph Bellamy and Charles Grandison Finney and what has been called 'Moderate Calvinism'. This school teaches that man is only fallen in certain parts which do not include his natural abilities. Any man is thus able to please God in his own strength—if he wants. Joseph Bellamy, the father of this movement, even claims, as if the dreadful fall of man in Eden had never taken place, that man is perfectly able to keep the whole Law.[4] His English counterpart Andrew Fuller, who called himself a 'strict Calvinist', whispers in our ear that even our moral abilities have not been marred by the fall. We have the same power to believe as we have to disbelieve;[5] indeed, he can even say that fallen man is still not 'unable in every respect' or 'totally unable' to believe in Christ.[6] When doughty Dan Taylor took the latter to task on this point, Fuller replied:

> Though Mr T. talks of men as having 'no will or power to believe in Christ, nor any concern in the matter' prior to the Spirit's work, (XII. 23.) yet that is what I have never affirmed. On the contrary, I maintain that men

[4] *True Religion Delineated,* p. 93 and passim.
[5] *Works,* III, Moral Inability, p. 768.
[6] *Works,* II, Reply to Mr Button, p. 438.

19

have the same power, strictly speaking, before they are wrought upon by the Holy Spirit, as after; and before conversion as after; that the work of the Spirit endows us with no new rational powers that are necessary to moral agency.[7]

Fuller was looking for a method to allow man the ability to respond to God's offer of grace. His way of using his allegedly unfallen 'rational powers' was to argue that if a man were really dead in trespasses and sin, God could not demand of him that he should wake up and serve Him. But here, Fuller's rational powers fail him totally. Instead of concluding that God does not demand of dead man that he raises himself from the dead and follows Christ, he argues that man cannot be totally dead after all and this is why God can still offer him salvation which he has the ability to accept. Indeed, Fuller's main theme in his notorious book with the misleading title *The Gospel Worthy of all Acceptation,* a rehash of Bellamy's major work, argues:

> If sinners were naturally and absolutely unable to believe in Christ, they would be equally unable to disbelieve; for it requires the

---

[7] *Works,* II, The Reality and Efficiency of Divine Grace, pp. 546, 547 fn.

same powers to reject as to embrace. And, in this case there would be no room for an inability of another kind: a body is equally unable to do evil as to do good; and a man naturally and absolutely blind could not be guilty of shutting his eyes against the light.

One can only conclude that Fuller argues in this way because he believes that man's reason is not fallen, though his reasoning might be, and that he has a far higher view of man than that revealed in Scripture. Fuller never answers the question satisfactorily from a Biblical perspective, what, if some choose and others do not, moves the one to choose and other to reject? Surely, this cannot be because some are naturally more godly than others? Furthermore how can an evangelist in the light of Scripture which says, The heart is deceitful above all things, and desperately wicked: who can know it?' nevertheless strive to convince sinners that of themselves they both can and must rightly choose God.

Fuller's way out of this dilemma is based on his understanding of the so-called moral government principle, which he combines with the smattering of theology which he picked up through reading Bellamy's *True Religion Delineated.* Fuller, an ex-wrestler and pastor of a Hyper-Calvinist, Antinomian church before adopting even stranger theological views, claimed that we must think of God and the way of salvation in two ways. This is the first of many 'divisions' called for by advocates of the free offer.

First, God, as the moral Governor of the world, has prepared a full and sufficient salvation for all in the death of Christ. This is sufficient and full enough to convince all men of natural ability of what they ought to do. To believe on the Lord Jesus Christ for salvation, Fuller teaches, is the plain moral duty of all men based on the clear rational facts that Jesus Christ has atoned for their sins and presented them with a way back to God. Thus it is not incongruous to tell all men that Christ has died for all and that full salvation is there for the asking. This, says Fuller, demonstrates 'the good will of the Creator, whose tender mercies are over all his works.' This way of salvation shows man what, to use Fuller's own words 'ought to be effectual'.

But it does not work. Therefore the second way of viewing salvation is to see God, not as the moral pedagogue who points the way of duty but as the God of grace who saves when His moral persuasion fails. This theory of salvation, says Fuller, is not an 'ought' but an 'is'.[8] In other words, God has provided an atonement sufficient for all which becomes ineffectual through man's

---

[8] *Works, III*, Of the Love of God, and Whether it extends to the Non-elect, p. 771.

stubbornness (Fuller's word) to do what he ought. Thus God, it would appear, as a last resort determines to save some and so, though the atonement is sufficient for all, it is only applied to some and is made effective in their case only. This view, in reality, is that propagated by the Scot's Cameron school through their French spokesman Moise Amyraut (1596-1664) who was contested by the bulk of English Puritans. Amyraldianism was well-defined in James MacGregor's essay *The Free Offer In the Westminster Confession,* where a footnote (editor's?) says:

> Amyraut boldly taught a hypothetical universalism, which was really a species of universal atonement. God willed by an antecedent decree that all men should be saved on condition of repentance and faith in Christ. He therefore sent Christ into the world to die for all men. But seeing that, left to themselves, none would repent and believe, He by a subsequent decree elected some as objects of the saving operation of His grace. These and these only are actually saved.[9]

---

[9] *Banner of Truth Magazine,* Number 82, 83, July-August 1970, p. 53. The quote is taken from Berkhof's *History of Christian Doctrine,* p. 190.

The Free Offer

Modern Fullerism

This bizarre Second-Chance or Two-Way Theory is behind much of the modern 'Moderate Calvinist' or 'Fullerite' preaching. It combines the free offer of salvation with the notion that believing in Christ is the natural duty of all men according to natural abilities. However, the Bible nowhere tells us of two routes for salvation, but rather that God has decreed one salvation for His elect through the exercise of His sovereign will. This will is the one, sole will of the Triune God and is the same throughout eternity regarding the salvation of those whom God graciously calls His people. God is, in all His ways, changeless and immutable. Yet, sadly, modern evangelists of the Fullerite view favour the mixture presented by the New Divinity-Amyraldian schools which outdo even the Wesleys in their speculative fancy and radicalism. They feel that their system is saved by postulating at least two wills (note the divisions again) in the Godhead. The will to save all and the will to save some.

Are there not three Persons in the Trinity? they ask, and thus conclude that where three persons are, we can expect a plurality of wills. They set up a scenario which has everything in it to make a moving Father-Son soap opera relationship. Jesus, they claim, wishes to save everyone. But His Father is adamant. He will only save some. Thus the heavenly arches shudder as God the Father and God the Son quarrel over the salvation of sinners. This has led modern free offer preachers to develop their quite scandalous Tension Theory which postulates a tension between what the Godhead wants and what the Godhead does. Just as Michael contended with the devil over the body of Moses,[10] so Father and Son contend over the souls of sinners. There is an eternal tension in the Godhead concerning who should be saved.

This author first came across this view when reading through an article in the *Banner of Truth Magazine* entitled 'Preaching the Gospel to Sinners: 2' and subtitled 'The Will of God and our Preaching'. In it David Gay is struggling with his own problem of how God can desire the salvation of sinners whom He does not save. He finds his solution in saying:

> There are two aspects to the will of God. First, there is his absolute purpose and eternal decree. This is always fulfilled (Psalm 115:3; Psalm 135:6; Isaiah 46:10 etc.). Secondly, there is God's revealed will, his commands, invitations, the expression of his benevolence. Jesus said that he often desired that which God, clearly, had not decreed. God is perfectly consistent in this even though it is incomprehensible to us.

---

[10] Jude 9

The Free Offer

We are left to conclude that whereas Christ wishes to save all, the Father insists on only saving some. To back up his statement regarding the apparent incompatibility in the Father's and Son's wills, Gay informs his readers that when two paradoxical and irreconcilable truths appear in the Divine Council, we should humbly accept the fact that it is so.

Here we have the pure Dualism of Fuller who always maintained that the revealed will of God in Scripture is inferior to the secret will of God which is governed by Natural Law. The former only being used for a temporary purpose, but the latter being the true will of God. Thus, in order to boost his theory of the free offer, Gay must argue that there is not only a difference between the revealed and secret wills of God but also between God's desires in Christ and His decrees as the Father, it is no wonder that one reviewer, on summing up this new tension theology as expressed by Gay, called it 'blasphemous'.

Though Gay initially tells his readers that they must accept both God's will to elect for Himself a chosen people and His will in Christ to save all sinners, in his plea for a free and warranted offer of salvation to all, he totally drops the doctrine of God's decrees in his further argument and says concerning the salvation of sinners:

> But now I come to the heart of it. It is clear
> that God delights in the salvation of sinners. It

is proper to say that God takes pleasure in their salvation. But to say that does not go far enough; it falls short of the scriptural teaching on the free offer. The point is: Does God actually desire the salvation of sinners? Does he want sinners to be saved? And further, Does God desire the salvation of those who are reprobate?

This is the fundamental point at issue in the free offer. John Murray put it this way: 'It would appear that the real point in dispute in connection with the free offer of the gospel is whether it can properly be said that God desires the salvation of all men.'

I assert that this is the heart of the matter. Does God desire the salvation of all men? The answer is, Yes! Therefore we must, in our preaching, declare indiscriminately to all our hearers that God desires to see them saved. Further, we are preaching the gospel to sinners properly, only when we are convinced of the truth of such a desire in God and say so very clearly. We can only persuade sinners to be reconciled to God when we are persuaded that God not only delights in their salvation, but he actually desires it.

The Free Offer

Gay, who is obviously struggling to follow John Murray as will be made evident below, thus postulates two wills in the Godhead. The one referring to the atonement as the decreed will of God to adopt for Himself an elect people for whom Christ died. This 'will' Gay tactically leaves out so that he might preach as if God never granted an assured and certain salvation for those for whom Christ died. Instead, Gay teaches that what God does stands in stark contrast to what God *desires,* and it is what God desires which should be broadcast in evangelism, not what God does. Thus, after telling his readers in the *Banner of Truth Magazine* that there are two wills in the Godhead, we are really not surprised when David Gay reports in the *Evangelical Times* that the revealed Word of God is also self-contradictory and reveals two apparently contradictory 'gospels'. He has even the audacity to thrust forward Charles H. Spurgeon, citing him as one who believed that the testimony of Scripture is irreconcilable with itself.[11] This writer was once very familiar with the works of Spurgeon but never gained the impression that he believed God's word to reflect two different gospels. As with the alleged wills of God, Gay, is arguing for a dualism in Scripture, both forms of which we must accept.

---

[11] *Evangelical Times,* Gay's review of Iain Murray's *Spurgeon v. Hyper-Calvinism,* Aug, 1996, p.19.

Then, yet again, Gay shows his willingness to drop his own advice that both 'gospels' must be accepted and drops the Scriptural passages which refer to Christ's particular atonement. This leaves him free to preach to persuade men according to their natural abilities to repent and believe on the purely rational grounds that God, if He is God, must desire it.

Though Gay, as also John Murray, may not be aware of it, the dual wills and dual gospels teaching that give them the unction to preach the so-called 'free offer' are really based on the Moral Government Theory of Hugo Grotius as understood by Fuller. Grotius and Fuller teach that there are two principle laws by which man must live, the Natural (permanent) Law and the Revealed (temporary) Law. Gay redesigns this Dual Law Theory, one inferior to the other, to argue that the supposedly 'secret' law of God regarding His decrees, must fade away before the revealed law of God which Gay interprets in universal terms.[12]

Rather than believe this rationalistic liberalism, we can safely note that the Scriptures are the only revelation we have from God and though Fuller and his followers claim that Natural Law is superior even to God, the Scriptures tell us that God rules Natural Law and uses it to show us that man is inexcusable in rejecting God in Nature but that Nature condemns him and can never save him. Paul's

[12] See page 33ff. for a fuller description of Grotian teaching.

The Free Offer

teaching in Romans chapters 1 and 2 is a clear example of this.

That which Gay sees as man's passport to salvation is that which damns him and lays open the need for a better way and a more perfect atonement. This way, as will be outlined later, is that God not only provides salvation for His chosen ones; He procures and secures it.

John Murray and the Free Offer

As Gay and most modern adherents of the free offer on the so-called 'Moderate Calvinist' side appeal to the writings of John Murray as grounds for their departure from traditional, Biblical views of the Atonement, it will help to understand the basic dualism of this system by analysing Murray's reasoning in coming to his free offer position.

John Murray, writing in his *The Atonement and the Free Offer of the Gospel,* bases his appeal for a free offer on Christ's words in Luke 24:47, 'repentance and remission of sins should be preached in his name among all nations, beginning at Jerusalem.' This is a great Scriptural truth though it hardly draws a demarcation line between free offer people and those who believe the practice to be unbiblical. Richard Davis, John Gill, William Huntington, Robert Hawker, William Gadsby and many more whom the Fuller-Gay-Murray lobbyists would throw out of the Parliament of the Saints, were great preachers of repentance, faith and righteousness and were instrumental in the salvation of thousands. Yet they are considered Antinomians and Hyper-Calvinists because they do not understand the offer in the highly liberal terms presented by such as Gay and Murray.

Yet, after stating what would delight the heart of any Christian, and affirming that this gospel-preaching has its authority in the atonement, Murray spoils his essay by declaring:

'Unto all the nations' bespeaks universality. And since repentance is redolent of the gospel, the universality of the demand for repentance implies the universal overture of grace.

From one gospel to two
Thus, instead of merely taking Luke 24:47 at its word and recommending the preaching of repentance and the forgiveness of sins, Murray seems to be saying that as repentance is commanded of all, grace will be provided for all so that all might repent through the merits of a universal atonement. It would further appear that Murray, in his free offer of grace to all mankind, is suggesting that automatically all become partakers of grace as they come under the universal call to repent. Murray, however, does not follow up such a dogmatic statement with simple reasoning from Scriptures but goes into philosophical

The Free Offer

niceties which, when boiled down to facts, merely indicate his own lack of conviction and system, apart from the fact that he must hang on to his free offer beliefs at all costs. He thus begins to differentiate radically as to the nature and scope of the gospel, maintaining that there is 'a certain universalism belonging to the redemptive events that lays the basis for and warrants the universal proclamation. In other words, the extension in proclamation cannot be divorced from the question of extent.' The key words here to note are 'a certain universalism' and 'extent'. Murray is preparing the way for a two-gospels theory, one gospel being universal and the other of limited extent, however, neither of them are, in fact, the gospel that he freely offers.

One design of the atonement, according to Murray, is that the non-elect receive universal and indiscriminate benefits from Christ's redemptive work. Christ is in control of the world as a dispenser of good and He enables believers to 'do good to all men' so that order, equity, benevolence and mercy can reign on earth. Here, Murray is supported by the sound exegesis of saints throughout all ages and in all church fellowships. Thus we find that early 17th century John Davenant, Anglican co-compiler of the Five Points of Calvinism and Baptist John Gill of the following century taught exactly the same. However, it is again Murray's own private interpretation of such a fact which causes concern. In establishing what theologians usually call 'common grace' i.e. God's benevolent acts to all men through the merits of Christ's work on the cross,

Murray concludes that, 'there is a gospel of salvation proclaimed to all without distinction.' This is the gospel of God's universal love to mankind. At last we have it! This is apparently the free offer.

It must be queried whether such a gospel can really be called a gospel of salvation. And indeed, once Murray has established the alleged universal love to all, he begins to differentiate again and argue that the atonement, 'has an entirely different reference to the elect' leading to a 'radical differentiation'. Though the non-elect accrue benefits from the atonement they are not atoned for as the atonement was not designed for them. There is, Murray tells us, a 'differentiation' in God's love. He loves mankind universally and beneficially but loves His elect with a higher love savingly.

Murray must have realised that he was making it more and more difficult for his readers to understand what a 'free offer' of the gospel had to do with all this. Which of Murray's gospels is to be offered freely? The indiscriminate gospel of God's love to all mankind or the discriminate gospel to the elect? Taking the limited application of the gospel first, Murray accepts that it is the true doctrine but does not make this the contents of his free offer arguing nebulously that the term has nothing to do with offering the possibility or opportunity of salvation but with salvation itself. Secondly, Murray complicates the issue further by arguing that 'it is not the general love of

33

The Free Offer

God to all mankind, the love manifested in the gifts of general providence, that is offered to men in the gospel.'

From two gospels to three

Thus the gospel which is to be freely offered is not the gospel of election, nor the gospel of universal love. Murray, however, has yet another gospel. 'Sinners', he tells us, 'are not asked to believe that God or Christ loves them with a differentiating love. The gospel simply demands that they come to Christ and commit themselves to him.' Murray argues that as Christ is salvation it is Christ who must be offered. This is the gospel which is to be offered to all men. Murray takes this step because he believes that 'It cannot be declared to men indiscriminately that, in the proper sense of the term, Christ died for them.' In teaching, however, that the free offer is an offer of Christ, Murray has not explained who Christ is or what Christ's work is. Nor has he explained how salvation might be appropriated through the preaching of the free offer. Murray has *not* introduced Christ to the sinner. He has not given the grounds of a sinner's salvation.

This view of the 'free offer' as a third-choice gospel, obviously raises more questions than it answers. It does not explain what place in the gospel repentance plays although it is the gospel of repentance that led Murray on to his free offer theology. Must repentance precede faith and what is meant by 'offering Christ'? If a description of Christ's work is not at least part of the contents of the gospel offered, what sense is there in proclaiming an unknown Saviour?

Not one Divine will but two

Murray is not unaware of the confusion he has caused. He therefore seeks to answer some of the many questions raised by his theory in his essay *The Free Offer of the Gospel* presented before the Fifteenth General Assembly of the Orthodox Presbyterian Church in 1948.[13] The real point of dispute concerning the free offer, he argues is 'can it properly be said that God desires the salvation of all men?' Murray concludes that whereas this is the case with the *revealed will* of God, it is not the case with the *decretive or secret will of God.* So we note again, that dominant feature of all so-called Moderate Calvinist free offer enthusiasts, namely that they must postulate two wills in the Godhead.

Rather than assist our understanding of the free offer issue, Murray has complicated the matter further. He presents us with a plurality of contradictory gospels and two highly contradictory wills of God. Murray seems to be arguing that, leaving the Fall aside, God would wish all to be saved, but in view of the Fall and His subsequent will to save at least some, though none deserve it, God now only

---

[13] Re-published by Banner of Truth Trust in vol. IV of the *Collected Writings of John Murray,* 1982.

desires His elect to be saved. This point would be acceptable to most Calvinists but Murray draws conclusions from it hardly warranted by his premise. He believes that the gospel of salvation must be offered universally to all mankind in accordance with God's *original desire* for all to be saved and not His *decreed desire* to save some. In order to prove that his deduction is correct, Murray quotes Matthew 5:44-48:

> But I say unto you, Love your enemies, bless them that hate you, and pray for them which despitefully use you, and persecute you. That ye may be the children of your Father which is in heaven: for he maketh his sun to rise on the evil and on the good, and sendeth rain on the just and on the unjust. For if ye love them which love you, what reward have ye? do not even the publicans the same? And if ye salute your brethren only, what do ye more than others? do not even the publicans so? Be ye therefore perfect, even as your Father which is in heaven is perfect.

The Free Offer gospel is a cut-down gospel

This passage, Murray argues, 'tells us something regarding God's benevolence that has bearing upon all manifestations of divine grace.' He backs up this conclusion with quotes from Acts 14:17; Deuteronomy 5:29, 32:29; Psalm 81:13ff. and Isaiah 48:18; Matthew 23:37; Luke 13:34 and Ezekiel 18:23, 32; 33:11. All these passages, however, merely imply that God shows benevolence (Murray's word) to the just and the unjust and that He has no delight in the death of the wicked. If this is the free offer gospel, it falls far short of the full gospel of salvation in God's effectual call of the elect and thus it may be a gospel but it is not the full gospel.

Not two wills but three

Next, Murray deals with Isaiah 45:22, 'Look unto me, and be ye saved, all the ends of the earth: for I am God, and there is none else.' At last Murray has found a text which has to do with salvation and that on a worldwide scale. Two things must be noted, however. Rather than salvation being *offered* here, God is *commanding*. The people are *ordered* to assemble (v. 20), tell, bring (v. 21) and look (v. 22). They are *told* what will happen if they obey and what will happen if they do not obey. Those that disobey will be ashamed and confounded (vv. 16, 24) and those that obey will be saved (vv. 17, 22). Here we have a clear testimony to the fact that God's call to the world is a *discriminating call.* Furthermore, the entire message of these chapters in Isaiah is to show that God upholds His elect and He has called them by their name to be His (43:1; 44:1). They shall be saved for ever and their enemies will be condemned. Murray argues that the universality of the command (he is suddenly writing about commands and not offers) is apparent from the expression 'all the ends of the earth'. He concludes that this illustrates 'the will that all should turn to him and be saved' and adds, 'While, on the one hand, he has not *decretively willed* that all should be saved, yet he declares unequivocally that it is his will and, *impliedly,* his pleasure that all turn and be saved.' So now we find that God has not two, but three radically different wills concerning man's salvation. He has an *original will to* save all, a *decretive will to* save some and an *implied will* that all will turn to him voluntarily (?) and be saved.

Apart from totally denying the immutability of God, this argument wrenches the text from its context. From Isaiah 40 onwards, starting with those moving words, 'Comfort ye, comfort ye my people, saith your God,' we are faced with the inner mysteries of the gospel, revealing the love of God for the Church for whom He allowed His Son, the Suffering Servant (42:1) to die out of pure love. In other words, the whole witness of these chapters is diametrically opposed to Murray's exegesis. The gospel which is here expounded is one of discerning, discriminating love, a gospel which Murray refuses to accept as the gospel which is to be offered freely to all.

Is saving grace universal or particular?

Is Murray arguing for a universal grace to match the universal call to repentance and remission of sins or a discriminating, saving grace? Murray seems to halt permanently between these two opinions. In his closing words, however, Murray comes down firmly on the former proposition and declares:

> The full and free offer of the gospel is a grace bestowed upon all. Such grace is necessarily a manifestation of love or lovingkindness in the heart of God. And this lovingkindness is revealed to be of a character or kind that is correspondent with the grace bestowed. The grace offered is nothing less than salvation in its richness and fulness.

This is an expression that would please the most ardent Arminian and quite does away with the doctrine of election and the fact that God saves some but passes by others. Murray, however, claims to be a Calvinist. One can only question why he sticks tenaciously to a phrase, the defence of which leads him to empty the gospel of its most important features, according to orthodox Calvinists, in order to make it acceptable to a mass audience. Once the self-contradictory way Murray has chosen is embarked upon, it opens the door to more and more difficulties. Murray's argument that one must offer Christ but not Christ's message is one of them. Curt Daniel, in his work *Hyper-Calvinism and John Gill,* views this interpretation of the gospel as being typically Antinomian. He says of Saltmarsh, whom he believes is both a Hyper-Calvinist and an Antinomian, 'With typical Antinomian boldness of expression Saltmarsh wrote, "The Gospel is Christ revealed. The Gospel is Christ himself."'[14] obviously believing that a preacher who is not prepared to outline his gospel further is not preaching the free offer. Later Daniel quotes Murray's summary of the gospel as 'offering Christ' and links him with Saltmarsh.[15] The fact is, as soon as one starts offering a gospel freely that is void of content and avoids controversial points, one is in danger of being regarded as a heretic by all sides. What is very evident from Murray's muddled reasoning is that, in order to plead for a free offer of saving grace for all, he has to ignore both the decrees of God and the traditional, biblical doctrine of the atonement of Christ.

---

[14] *Hyper-Calvinism and John Gill,* p. 388.
[15] Ibid, p. 410.

Part Two

The Nature And Scope Of The Atonement

To a student of church history and church heresy, such a mixed-up view of various theories of decrees and atonements and the Arian and Socinian views which so often go with them comes as no surprise. The surprise is when they come from the Calvinist quarter which has always insisted, until the days of Fuller at least, on a particular atonement, on the invincible work of the Spirit in turning man from damnation to salvation and on the fact that Christ's atonement was not in vain and those whom He aimed to save are saved. The faulty theory of the Atonement which underlines the entire reasoning of Wesley, but to a greater extent Fuller, Gay and Murray emerged in the Dark Ages of Rome when Biblical doctrine, in God's Providence, lost control of the churches and

The Free Offer

Scholastic scepticism and speculation took hold of the imagination of church leaders who were unspiritual men.

Abelard's alternative atonement

Although there has been nothing under the sun in new heresies since Satan's rebellion and man first wished to become as gods, the main break away from the Biblical doctrine of the atonement was made by Pierre de Palais (1079-1142), better known as Abelard, the name he assumed. He maintained that the doctrine that Christ died the just for the unjust and paid the penalty for His elect's sins was immoral. Not too saintly to father the child of the woman he refused to marry, Abelard told the world that God could not have been so wicked as to plan the death of His Son as the grounds for forgiving sin. God is love and demands no satisfaction to help Him forgive penitent sinners. Christ's aim, he believed, was to assert a sound moral influence on man, proving divine love by assuming our nature and living an exemplary life even to the point of death. It is a contemplation of this great love that awakens love in our hearts and it is this love given back to God which is the basis for forgiveness of sins. As a result of this act, believers can live freely in obedience to God, motivated by love in their hearts. This is still the gospel of most free offer holders who proclaim 'God loves you, you must love Him back.'

Abelard brought into theology an entirely new picture of God, a God who is so lost in His attributes, that His personality disappears and He becomes a mere moral philosophy. His is a God so motivated by love that He pays attention neither to His own justice nor His own holiness and completely fails to answer the question posed by Anselm, 'Why did God become man?' Rather than it being a cruel thing for God to reconcile sinners to Himself through the vicarious, voluntary death of Christ, Abelard's theory of a God who allows His Son to suffer and die the death of a criminal when He could have morally influenced the sinner in a thousand other, safer, ways, seems cruel indeed. Abelard, too, must have had a very imperfect view of the grip sin has on man if he thought that an example alone, no matter how good, might cause him to live a life pleasing to God.

The Socinians follow suit
The followers of Faustus Socinus (1539-1604), were delighted with the views of Abelard which helped support their own brand of heresy. They too, had no real teaching of the Trinity, believing that the Holy Spirit was a mere divine influence and that Christ was a man born in time. They, as Abelard, denied outright the need for justice in God's dealing with sin. In their view, God is not limited in His forgiveness of sins to the work of Christ who bore them. He forgives freely, His love and mercy alone

determining who is to be forgiven. This display of love and mercy is granted to all who repent and obey. This example is given by Christ who shows us how to obey. The Socinians do not seem to have been in need of an example of how to repent. There is, therefore, no direct link between the death of Christ and redemption, indeed, redemption in the sense of ransom is rejected by the Socinians just as fervently as by Abelard. However, the Socinians did connect salvation in some way with Christ's death as they taught that after Christ died, God raised Him from the dead and gave Him the power to grant eternal life to those who accepted and followed His example.

The atonement as a political, governmental hypothesis
As both Abelard and Socinus were declared heretics by various church councils, those in public office thought it prudent to declare their opposition to this teaching, however they might sympathise with it. One Dutch statesman to protest in this way was Hugo Grotius whom we have already mentioned. This highly gifted man was born on 10 April, 1583 and became a pupil of Jan Uytenbogaert the Remonstrant leader and friend of Jacob Arminius. Grotius, alongside Jan van Oldenbarnveldt, strove to put into politics the Five Points of the Remonstrants (or Arminians) drawn up by Uytenbogaert and forty-six other ministers in 1610. Grotius' influence became so great that in 1614 he moved the Dutch Provinces

to pass a bill forbidding the preaching of the doctrines of grace. Grotius' policy was to seek peace by using political power to ban controversy. It was a most ineffectual way of exercising political reason and suppressing theological inquiry. Grotius' views were first published in a popular verse form and were eagerly taken up by the people and became the favourite shanties of many a ship's crew. These ditties were then worked out into a more academic form in 1627 which was published under the presumptuous title *de Veritate Religionis Christianae*. The most marked feature of the work is a trust in the validity and demonstrability of natural reason and the supremacy of Christian ethics as understood by the human mind rather than the revealed religion of the Bible. The three main thrusts of Grotius' argument are the high ideals of the Christian religion, the excellency of its rules of duty and the pre-eminence of Christ seen in His demonstrated ability to work miracles. The doctrines of the Trinity and the atonement are entirely absent from this work. They are superseded by the emphasis on the reasonableness of living the Christian life according to Christ's teaching .

Atonement by token
Grotius' political theory of the atonement is taken up in his *Defensio Fidel Cathoticae de Satisfactione Christ!* in which he strives to distance himself from Socinianism. His view of Christ's substitutionary, propitiating death is, however,

far nearer the Socinian view than the Biblical doctrine of redemption in Christ. He rejects, as the Socinians, any idea that Christ could take over the debts of another and provide payment for them in suffering as a ransom to settle the debtor's account regarding the broken law. God, he argues, is not to be viewed as a creditor but as an administrator, rector or benign governor. This divine administrator admittedly rules by laws but these laws are mere guides to right living and not absolute chains. As God does not demand that the law be obeyed in every particular, there is no need for a full satisfaction as if He did. Sin is always viewed by Grotians in a non-theological way as that which is contrary to 'the nature and fitness of things'. The Grotian idea of punishment is that it need not fit the crime as God's statute book is not absolute, laws and punishments being entirely at His benevolent discretion.

Christ, a benevolent probation officer

Rather than view Christ as the One who bore our exact penalty for breaking an absolute law, Grotius sees Him as a Probation Officer who gives God an opportunity of displaying benevolence to His Adam-like probationers. Christ's defence on behalf of the probationers is not what He has done to settle the score for them in the vicarious penal and jurat sense of ransom and remission. It is a plea for a removal of man's obligations through God's benevolent discretion. God, on His part, does not demand that the whole law, spirit and letter, be kept in any way by anyone but especially not His Son. He simply requires that some symbolic act or token should be performed in order to demonstrate that man's obligations have been cancelled. This token demonstration is claimed by Grotius as being a true satisfaction. He sees no point in Christ's putting Himself under the Law on our behalf, thus both fulfilling and establishing the law. Indeed, He lifts the entire doctrine of the atonement out of its spiritual, theological and historical background and places it in the airy-fairy world of moral philosophy and governmental speculation, shunning the revealed Word. Grotius can thus sum up the atonement by saying, There is no unconditional absolute; there is no payment of the exact debt; there is no substitution of a new obligation; but there is a remission in consequence of a precedent satisfaction.' This satisfaction was merely a nominal or token one, in Grotius' view, though he is quick to add that there was no inherent necessity for God to supply this, but He thought it was the best way to make sure that His administration was shown to be unquestionable. The main thrust of Grotius' theology is, however, that remission of sin comes via relaxing the law. Thus Christ's death was in no way retributive but, in accordance with Socinianism, merely exemplary.

The Free Offer

Christ's death a mere moral deterrent

Throughout all this teaching, which is claimed to be a metaphor explaining the common sense of Natural Law, the Persons of the Godhead, especially those of Christ and the Holy Spirit are almost phased out. The role of Christ, as in Socinianism, is reduced to that of a hero who is prepared to suffer in order to act as a deterrent for others so that they might shun evil. The truth expressed by the words of the well-known hymn 'There was no other good enough to pay the price of sin,' is entirely absent from Grotian thinking. Jesus, in Grotius' eyes, was merely a person of in-comparable dignity who was used as a symbolic means of demonstrating God's displeasure (the nearest the Governmentalists come to speaking of the wrath of God) and a moral deterrent and a demonstration of God's benevolence to man. In no way do we see Christ as providing a full and perfect compensation for man's wrongs as a result of his fallen nature.

Through emphasising Christ's death as a moral deterrent against man's future sins and an establishment of God's administration of the world as a result of Christ's example, there is no back-working in Grotius' theory and one wonders what happened to the world's sinners before Christ's deterrent death and how did God administer His rule of benevolence then?

Though Grotius constantly speaks of man's reason and logical powers, there is no reason or logic whatsoever in

Governmentalist politico-theology. The whole system is a mere dupe to frighten man off from doing wrong and to convince him that his sins do not really cut him off from God; they do not really need to be atoned for by a redemptive act which removes the deadly penalties under which he is eternally damned. Grotius' Christ never reaches even the dignity of the Socinian hero. He pictures Christ as performing an act to save sinners which was merely arbitrary and in no way compelling. Worse still, Christ is actually lowered to God's dupe as He suffered untold agonies where there was no jural or redemptive necessity to do so.

In presenting his view of salvation, Grotius' major mistake was in believing he could make religion popular by drawing it into the realms of political and philosophic thought, redefining the theological terms of the Bible and traditional theology to make them appeal to natural reason. Even here, Grotius failed as his vocabulary, apart from his seamen's yarns, is more reminiscent of the ancient Greeks than the language of the party he sided with in his time as Advocate General of the Dutch Provinces. For a statesman, Grotius is surprisingly unconcerned with law and order as he portrays God as not being so much concerned with a broken law and a reign of justice as in demonstrating benign benevolence. His naive belief is that a God who does not want to be taken seriously must be a good God.

The Free Offer

An atonement at discount prices

Grotius, in wishing to demonstrate the loving nature of God, nowhere reaches the expression of love found in Christ's act of redemption. There is no union of Christ with His people in Grotius' theology and no absolute identification. Christ did not go the whole way to save the otherwise unsavable. He did not stand where we stood in having our sins imputed to Him and we cannot stand where He stands by having Christ's righteousness placed on us. Indeed the Biblical doctrine of imputation is as foreign to Grotius as that of ransom. The Biblical account of the 'greater love' of Christ in redemption is seen by Grotius as a pictorial metaphor. Against this, he taught, that Christ's demonstration of suffering to deter man from sinning was not by placing the onus of fulfilling the law on Christ on our behalf as Christ was above the law all along and could not, because of His innocence, have ever really taken our place. This led him to deny that Christ paid the price demanded by God out of love to His people in order to balance the scales of God's just claims against them. He thus rejects the deep divine benevolence of Christ's vicarious act of loving grace for His Church and substitutes it for a veritable charade of a mocked-up, benignant token sacrifice which gives spectators no real clue to the great and crucial act it is supposed to signify.

All this teaching can be found more or less in the theology of Joseph Bellamy and his English disciple

Andrew Fuller and the works of our contemporaries influenced by him. Fuller looks on revealed religion of Scripture as secondary to Natural Law. He denies outright that through the atonement, the elects' sins are imputed to Christ who suffered for them and Christ's righteousness is imputed to elect sinners for their justification. Furthermore, Fuller denies the so-called commercial language of the Scriptures displayed in such blessed texts as 1 Corinthians 6:20; 7:23; 1 Peter 1:18, 19. For Fuller, the idea that Christ paid a price to redeem His people is at best a metaphor which has no exact parallels in Christ's or the Christian's experience. Indeed, most of our religious, i.e. Scriptural language, Fuller, like Grotius, sees as being merely metaphorical to be interpreted by our knowledge of 'the nature and fitness of things', i.e. Natural Law. Thus it is no surprise to find that Fuller, now proclaimed widely as the father of the free offer dogma and even the father of the modern missionary movement, taught that Christ did not put Himself under the Law on the sinner's behalf but satisfied God's demands of the law by a mere token fulfilment.

Natural Law versus divine will

Grotius distinguishes between the divine will and Natural Law. The latter is ever fixed and unchangeable but this is not the case with the divine will. God, unlike Natural Law, does not will a thing to be because it is just but decrees that a thing is just because He wills it. Though Natural Law is permanent, revealed law, which reflects the divine will (Governmentalists insist on spelling Natural Law with capitals but the divine law in small letters) is only as permanent as God wishes it to be and is, in fact, merely a metaphorical demonstration and illustration of Natural Law, requiring human reason to interpret it, in this way removing the kernel or spirit of a law from its outer shell or letter.

True to his desire to combine theology with theories of statesmanship, Grotius outlined his views concerning divine revelation and the Word of God in his Latin treatise on war and peace, *de Jure Belli et Pads,* written in 1625. The Laws of Nature, he argues, are so infinite, unalterable and fixed that even God could not change them as He is subject to them Himself.

Furthermore, all God's creation reflect these laws as God has no other alternative but to work according to them. Rational man is able to comprehend these laws by means of *a priori* and *a posteriori* reasoning. The laws can be deduced a *priori* from the conception of human nature itself.

Though Grotius wrote at a time of acute political and religious unrest, his optimism concerning the perfections of human nature was boundless and he really thought that human reason could accept and understand the underlying nature and fitness of the universe as the best of all possible creations. Grotius found this basic conviction in man—one could almost call it instinct—strengthened a *posteriori* as what he called 'the more civilised nations' were unanimous in their respect for and adherence to Natural Law. This has its relevance, Grotius believed, in interpreting the Scriptures, which often seem to contradict human reason. Grotius even went further by affirming that every man has not only an awareness of these eternal laws but has a natural feeling of duty towards them.

Here we see the seeds sown which have produced the free offer, duty-faith weeds of modern evangelism. Man's eyes, we are to believe, are naturally open to his predicament and the way of salvation is clear before him, all he needs is encouragement from the gospel to change his moral disposition. The fact that he knows through the gospel that God desires his salvation, should induce in him a love for Christ which further induces his salvation.

A gospel that ignores sin and the grace of God to deal with it

Such a view is to confuse law with gospel and the work of Moses with that of Christ. In his great work *Christ Alone Exalted,* Tobias Crisp (1600-1643), that great winner of souls, tackles Grotian-like Christian Pharisees and explains to them the difference between a blind sinner and one whose eyes have been open:

The Free Offer

The first of all these kinds of the grace of God, that he doth ever bestow upon a person, is, The opening his eyes to see himself filthy, and to see what he is: here begins a closing with Christ, to see a need of him, and to see the usefulness of him being received. Now mark this great business, of the opening of the eyes of a person, and you shall see he is a way unto it, Isaiah 42:6. There the Father doth treat with Christ, and in his treaty he speaks thus to him, 'I will give thee for a covenant to the people, to open the blind eyes.' You see this, it is Christ that must open the blind eyes of men. Beloved, men are mistaken that think that the law makes them to see their own vileness; for a gracious sight of our vileness is the only work of Christ. The law is a looking-glass, able to represent the filthiness of a person; but the law gives not eyes to see that filthiness: bring a looking-glass and set it before a blind man, he seeth no more spots in his face than if he had none at all; though the glass be a good glass, yet the glass cannot give eyes; yet, if he had eyes, the glass might represent his filthiness. The apostle James compares the law to a looking-glass, and that is all the law can do, to have a faculty to represent; but it doth not give a faculty to see what it doth represent: it is

Christ alone that doth open the eyes of men, to behold their own vileness and filthiness; and when Christ will open the eyes, then a man shall see himself what he is.[16]

Thus any true doctrine of atonement on which we can build any truly Scriptural doctrine of preaching and evangelism must take into account the depths of man's sin, how God in Christ dealt with it and how this can be applied to sinful creatures. In other words, how dead bones can be made alive.

No law substitute for a full atonement of grace
Neither Grotius, Wesley, Fuller, Gay nor Murray provide a solution to the problem of law, sin and the righteousness necessary to fulfil the law. The Moralists say that Christ's example should prompt us to love Him and the Governmentalists tell us that the fact of Christ's deterrent death ought to frighten us into obedience. Fuller appeals more to law but to the wrong one. He takes man's gaze from the atonement which is necessary for the Divine Law to be fulfilled and places it on a Moral or Natural Law which, for him, is not a covenant of works and claims that it is a mere metaphor to tell the criminal (rather than the

[16] See Tobias Crisp Series, Issue 1, *Christ the Only Way,* Christian Bookshop, 21 Queen Street, Ossett, West Yorkshire WF5 8AS, 1995, p. 29.

sinner) to love Christ as if he had never apostatised and in fulfilling this duty he will be saved.[17] Love + Fear = Duty + Salvation in Fullerism but this is not one whit better than the mock-gospel Grotius, and the New Divinity theorists give us. It does not deal with the guilt of man. It does not deal with sin as sin and does not even begin to answer the question of how a man may get right with an angry God. Indeed, the vast majority of free offer writers depict God as being narrowly but lovingly benevolent to the point of exhibiting blindness to justice and mercy. Fuller subjectifies the atonement as he teaches that actual at-one-ment is instigated by personal repentance and faith. He thus robs the atonement of its objective, historical display of mercy in which Christ covered His bride's sins there and then on the cross. The atonement is thus also robbed of the very benevolence of which Fuller boasts. Fuller and his modern followers equally rob the atonement of its justice as they deny that it was at Calvary that the ransom was paid once and for all time.

A reformation of our so-called Reformed churches needed

The interest of the churches throughout the ages has tended to highlight certain doctrines or certain heresies at certain times. Traditionally it has been different views of church order and the ordinances which have separated true

---

[17] The Gospel Worthy of All Acceptation, *Works,* Vol. II, pp. 375, 376.

evangelicals from one another denomination-wise: a fact that has not prevented true Christians experiencing real fellowship in the Lord on a private 'inner church' level or in joint evangelistic enterprises. Today rifts between the brethren appear to be growing deeper as modern highly influential Neo-evangelicals maintain that he alone preaches the atoning blood of Christ who teaches it as a mere provision of God which gains its efficacy through reception. In other words, God's provision in the atonement does not secure salvation but the appropriation of it by the human agent does. Nowadays, those who were once rightly considered heretics in the churches are usurping the mantle of orthodoxy and proclaiming that holders of traditional views of the atonement are Hyper-Calvinists and Antinomians and thus criminals in God's eyes and unworthy of being given the right hand of fellowship. Such radicals who are rapidly becoming the modern evangelical establishment are bringing in theories of evangelism that are void of any objectivity and certainly void of Scriptural backing. It is thus of the utmost importance that we consider this fundamental doctrine of our faith, the atone-ment, in order to see if our feet really stand on the Rock of Ages who is faith's only foundation. Unless we are right about the atonement, we can never presume to preach the gospel sufficiently and efficiently. A new Reformation of our churches is needed.

The Free Offer

Finding the right word for the right doctrine

When William Tindale began work on his translation of the Bible around 1525, he found the English language at times most inappropriate for the task. There was very little of what might be called the language of Zion in English as the current Bible was in the Latin words of the Vulgate, or in the French language, of which many monks and priests were as ignorant as the common people. As it was deemed an evil thing by the Roman Catholic hierarchy for the common people to have the Bible in their own language, any words to do with Scriptural doctrines were highly Latinized and tainted with Roman superstition. Wycliffe's translation had had a limited circulation since the late 14th century but that work had received the full enmity of the Roman Church. Archbishop Arundel had declared Wycliffe to be a child of the devil and the offspring of Anti-Christ who 'crowned his wickedness by translating the Scriptures into the mother tongue.' In 1408, a general excommunication against readers of Wycliffe's Bible and against would-be translators of the Bible into English was proclaimed. By 1525, however, the English language was establishing itself as a language of poetry and prose and had changed radically during the previous hundred years. Wycliffe's language had become archaic and, as it was a mere translation of the Vulgate, it still contained Romanizing elements which dimmed the full meaning of Scripture.

Tindale, working from the original languages found it particularly difficult to translate words to do with atonement, reconciliation, propitiation, expiation and justification which are all closely linked in meaning. Perhaps his eagerness to make the translation really English caused him to reject Latin words which could have been employed usefully. Tindale looked for words which expressed matters of fact rather than use the current literary English vocabulary of fable, fantasy and fairy story. He could therefore say:

> I had no man to counterfet neither was holpe
> with englysshe of eny that had interpreted the
> same orsoche lyke things in the scripture
> before tyme.

Though one initial problem for Tindale was the paucity of good Middle English words suitable for depicting doctrine, an equal problem was the flood of new words coming into the language to supplement them. As Latin words vied with French, Scandinavian and Saxon words, a whole host of synonyms emerged, many of these quickly taking on new meanings. Our modern English language has to struggle even harder with this problem today as we can often find a large number of words to translate a Hebrew or Greek word but even then, the exact meaning of the original may not be given or understood absolutely

The Free Offer

correctly. It may surprise readers to find that one single Hebrew root word *kipper* with its derivations, Greek equivalents and word-families may be translated by either 'atonement', 'cover', 'mercy', 'grace', 'pardon', 'satisfaction', 'reconciliation' and even, and perhaps especially, 'ransom'. Theologians are sometimes at loggerheads over the meaning of the words 'expiation' and 'propitiation' but these words must be added to the same list.

God provides an at-one-ment with Himself
The first synonym mentioned above, atonement, is of particular interest as it was coined by Tindale himself to help get over translation difficulties. His God-led understanding of the words *kipper* and *hilasterion* was that they pointed to God's initiative in Salvation, to a full and entire work of the triune God in making a total satisfaction for sin by providing a complete substitution, which was a once-and-for-all act procuring everlasting salvation for the repentant sinner. The Roman Catholic Church viewed the atonement as reconciliation being made to God for man's guilt or original sin but not for the penalty of sin which had to be worked off by works of special merit and penance. This left the reconciled without true union with Christ and with Christ's work only half done. This error led Tindale to realise that the entire Biblical teaching was concerned with man becoming fully accepted in the Beloved, and thus

becoming one with God. Christ's reconciling death, he therefore saw, was an at-one-ment with God and promptly used the word to express both the Old and New Testament words to do with a man becoming right with God through an expiatory sacrifice at God's initiative.

God covers the sinner's shame

The word-family *kipper* is used in the Old Testament in conjunction with offerings to plead for mercy, to appease God, to grant blood money as an equivalent for physical harm done and to renew and keep up the covenant with God by which He has chosen a special people to serve Him and have fellowship with Him.[18] The root meaning of the word here is 'to cover'. The sins of the people are covered over and where this is performed in faith to God, He promises to remember these sins no more. Nowhere is this truth so beautifully put as in Ezekiel 16 where the prophet describes the birth of God's people, born in sin and squalor and virtually thrown away as unwanted, yet covered by God's own skirt. The cast-away child is washed, cleansed of blood, anointed and clothed in majesty by the grace of God. Zechariah tells us of Joshua as a type of the Church whose iniquities are put away and new garments given him. Isaiah saw clearly the atoning work of the Messiah with the eye of faith and could exclaim, 'I will greatly rejoice in the Lord, my soul shall be joyful in my God for he hath clothed

---

[18] Leviticus 1:4; 4:20; 16:10; Exodus 29:36; Numbers 5:8; Ezekiel 43:20 ff..

me with the garments of salvation, he hath covered me with the robe of righteousness' (61:10). David can say, 'Blessed is he whose transgression is forgiven, whose sin is covered,' and goes on to call the Lord his hiding-place (Psalm 32). Here, again, is a preview of the once-and-for-all-time sacrifice of Christ in whom our sinful life is hidden in God and He deals with us as new creatures (Colossians 3:3).

Perhaps the most significant passage in the Old Testament where the word 'atonement' is used is that referring to the Day of Atonement *(Yom Kippur)*. After a proscribed ten days of national preparation the High Priest would enter the holy place[19] to make a sin offering for himself and his people. After this was completed, the people's sins were symbolically laid on a scapegoat and sent away 'by the hand of a fit man into the wilderness: and the goat shall bear upon him all their iniquities unto a land not inhabited: and he shall let go the goat in the wilderness.'[20] All this, the writer to the Hebrews tells us, was a shadow or type of things to come. It was a forerunner of the day when the veil of the Temple should be rent for ever and Christ would take up His holy work as the fit man, the God-Man who would bear our sins away in that great and glorious never to be repeated action on the cross. The writer to the Hebrews argues that earthly priests come and go as they must all die but our great High Priest has gained

[19] The Temple was not built at the time of the law-giving.
[20] Leviticus 16:21, 22.

for us eternal access to God's holy abode and ever makes intercession for us there (chapter 7).

God provides a sacrifice for sanctification

In the Old Testament previews of the work of Christ, the ransoming work of sacrificial blood is given pre-eminence. The blood of the sacrificial victim shed is the sign of God's covenant with man to show that He is ever prepared to grant atonement and forgiveness for His people. The Old Testament saints were ransomed by sacrifices which were mere pointers to the great sacrifice to come which would be absolute and perfect in its power, working *from eternity* both backwards and forwards in history, covering the sins of the elect in all ages. Thus when Christians worship their Saviour, they draw nigh to 'Jesus the mediator of the new covenant, and to the blood of sprinkling, that speaketh better things than that of Abel' (Hebrews 12:24).

This gives Peter every good reason to write to, 'the elect according to the foreknowledge of God the Father, through sanctification of the Spirit, unto obedience and sprinkling of the blood of Jesus Christ, ... which according to his abundant mercy hath begotten us again unto a lively hope by the resurrection of Jesus Christ from the dead, To an inheritance incorruptible, and undefiled, and that fadeth not away, reserved in heaven for you' (1 Peter 1:2-4).

The whole gospel is reflected in this passage. We see that redemption is for the elect of God, otherwise called the

The Free Offer

Bride of Christ. We note that the blood of Christ atones for the sins of this elect people and sanctifies them. This gives them hope which has been established through Christ's own resurrection. Here we also have a clear testimony of the perseverance of the saints which is incorruptibly and eternally vouchsafed.

At-one-ment is a work of the Trinity

The passage makes it also plain that salvation is a work of the whole Trinity. The Father sets the operation in action, the Spirit separates the elect from the world and Christ provides not only the victim, His obedient self, but He is the Offerer, giving Himself for His Bride. The fact that the entire Trinity was at work in the plan of redemption is very relevant in combating modern views of the atonement which suggest that either God shows two conflicting wills in the atonement, or Christ set His own will against His Father's in redeeming a people for Himself, or that Christ merely played the hero's part which was accepted with hindsight by God or that Christ was merely 'offered' by the Father as Abraham was prepared to offer Isaac. The emphasis on Christ's obedience and the blood money (ransom) paid also goes a long way in debunking modern Governmentalists and so-called Evangelical Calvinists who neither see the necessity of a full obedience to the law on Christ's part nor see the relevance of Christ dying for the elect and for none other. If Christ did not give His uttermost in obedience, utterly fulfilling the law on behalf of His Church, then He could not 'save them to the uttermost that come unto God by him' (Hebrews 7:25). Such passages as 1 Peter 1:2-4 and Hebrews 7:25 show that everything the whole Trinity decreed and did was entirely successful. To argue, as many free offer enthusiasts do, that Christ died in vain for the majority of those whose sins He atoned for with His blood, is denying that Christ gave His uttermost and placing the power of sinful man over that of our righteous God.

God provides a ransom

The Bible emphasises time and time again that the atonement was not only a means of releasing man from his sins but it also provided the instrument of this means in terms of ransom. Exodus 21:30-36 tells us that if a man has been gored to death by a dangerous ox, the owner of the ox can escape death by paying a ransom *(kopher)*. There was, however, no way of ransoming away death itself. Hence we read in Psalm 49:7 that no one can 'redeem his brother' from death, or 'give to God a ransom for him.' In Numbers 8:19 we find that the Levites are given to Aaron in order to provide a *kopher* for the children of Israel. By the time of the prophets, teaching concerning a ransomed New Covenant people had become widespread as revelation progressed. Isaiah could triumphantly say on viewing Christ's kingdom in chapter 35:10, 'And the ransomed of the Lord shall return, and come to Zion with songs and everlasting joy upon their heads: and they shall obtain joy and gladness, and sorrow and sighing shall flee away.' This is echoed by Jeremiah in his account of the calling in of elect Israel in 31:11 and God's promise to Hosea to ransom His people from the grave, saying, 'O death, I will be thy plagues; O grave, I will be thy destruction,' reminding us of 1 Corinthians 15:55, the plague of death being sin which is removed from the redeemed.

All this, of course, as the writer to the Hebrews tells us in great detail in chapters 7-10, is only a reflection of and pointer to the 'Lamb slain from the foundation of the world' (Revelation 13:8), which was outworked in the 'fulness of time' at Calvary. Though it happened in time, the Bible teaches that this sacrifice was beyond time, covering the entire history of salvation of the elect from Abel until the gathering in of the saints when Jesus comes in glory. We note that Christ's saving work is not a product of time. Salvation was prepared for the elect before the foundation of the world, i.e. in eternity (Matthew 25:34). Those for whom Christ died were loved by God in Christ before the foundation of the world (John 17:23 ff.). Indeed, the elect were chosen in union with Christ before the foundation of the world (Ephesians 1:4). Christ's atoning work was fore-ordained before the foundation of the world (1 Peter 1:20) and it is a Biblical truth that Christ was even slain from the foundation of the world (Revelation 13:8). All these Scriptural portions show that Christ in eternity has always being offering Himself for His elect who have always stood in union with Him. Calvary, according to the Scriptures, does not represent time but the *fulness* of time when eternity revealed itself to man drawing past, present and future, all time and all eternity into its scope, revealing the fact that God in Christ has always been reconciling His elect to Himself through the eternal atoning work of Christ, revealed and brought to its fulness in the fulness of time which therefore can rightly be called the fulness of eternity. This shows the great superiority of the Biblical all time and all eternity doctrine of the atonement over the atonement theories of the Moral Governmentalists and Fullerites who have really no Old Testament, pre-Calvary and eternal atonement as its moral persuasion can only work forwards in time and is dependable on man's agency for its fulfilment in time.

Christ is our ransom

In the New Testament the clear testimony is that the 'son of man came not to be ministered unto, but to minister and to give his life a ransom for many' (Matthew 20:28; Mark 10:45). Paul, in 1 Timothy 2:5, 6 explains that this is the essential part of Christ's mediatory work of reconciliation 'For there is one God, and one mediator between God and men, the man Christ Jesus; Who gave himself a ransom for sin, to be testified in due time.' The last phrase 'in due time' is not to be taken in its modern alternative meaning of

The Free Offer

'in time to come' but in its basic meaning of 'in the time that was due' or as Paul puts it in Galatians 4:4, 'But when the fulness of the time was come, God sent forth his Son, made of a woman, made under the law, To redeem them that were under the law, that we might receive the adoption of sons.' Again we see emphasised, so strongly, that Christ was not placed above the law as a privileged man but emptied Himself so thoroughly for our sakes that He came under the law to redeem those that were under the law. The modern rejection of the redemption doctrine of salvation by those who say that Christ's high position and dignity were respected too much by His Father to place Him under the law, is poison itself as it could never lift the death penalty from man. Thus the predominant theology of the free offer sect is based on an unfinished work of Christ on the cross. In Fuller's jargon, Christ did not cry out 'It is finished', but 'It is prepared and now left to you'. Thus, at the end of all doctrinal statements by Fuller, we find him telling us that salvation is set before us like a table well laid and now all that is required is that we sit down to eat The teaching that Christ's dignified superiority placed Him higher than the law and this dignity was accepted and given us as an 'as if status is good Fullerism but very bad theology. The Biblical way of salvation is that Christ had to become what we were in order to lift us up to be like Him. He voluntarily showed full obedience to the law. No other way was good enough for Him. This transformation was not a mere parable or allegory, nor was it merely judicial but it actually happened for our sakes. We can thus truly say, that we, as the Church of God, have been actually purchased by His blood (Acts 20:28); this means that we have actually been redeemed by His blood (Ephesians 1:7); we have actually been justified by His blood (Romans 5:9); we are actually sanctified by His blood (Hebrews 13:12) because our sins have been actually washed away by His blood (Revelation 1:5). This is all thanks be to God in Christ who actually bought us with a price (1 Corinthians 6:20; 7:23; 1 Peter 1:18 ff.).

This ransom was actual and not metaphorical

It is becoming fashionable in so-called 'Moderate Calvinism' to question the doctrine of literal redemption, i.e. that Christ was an actual ransom. The Apostle Peter was familiar with such critics and refers to them plainly and damnably in 2 Peter 2:1 saying, 'But there were false prophets also among the people, even as there shall be false prophets among you, who privily shall bring in damnable heresies, *even denying the Lord that bought them,* and bring upon themselves swift destruction.' In view of the modern Neo-evangelical theory, taken over from Grotian Fuller, that what they call 'commercial language[1] is at best to be understood metaphorically, we may quote 1 Peter 1:18-20 for a very matter-of-fact statement, 'For as much as ye know that ye were not redeemed with corruptible things, as silver and gold, from your vain conversation received by tradition from your fathers; But with the precious blood of Christ, as of a lamb without blemish and without spot: Who verily was foreordained before the foundation of the world but was manifest in these last times for you.' Now if Peter had said that God used all the riches, all the gold and silver, at His disposal to save us and gave His last penny to do so, this would be speaking metaphorically. Peter rejects such a symbolic language and comes down to plain facts. Christ was foreordained to be a ransom and a ransom He became. The price was to be paid in blood and, indeed, that is exactly how it was paid. If Christ had not paid the exact price under the obligations freely taken up before time-history began, we would be still in our sins or the slaves of some airy-fairy metaphorical, make-believe alternative.

This is the faith that was secured for Christ's redeemed in the atonement and if these truths are left out of the gospel then, however it is preached, it will not be preached properly.

Part Three

Free Offer Evangelism And Gospel Preaching

The folly of the Free Offer theory demonstrated from scripture

Most sects which break off from Christian orthodoxy do so because they have found a 'private interpretation or prophecy'[21] in one or two verses of Scripture which they feel have been in darkness until they came along. These sects also tend to offer spiritual benefits which they believe those from whom they departed did not enjoy. The following two texts are amongst the most often quoted by the free offer enthusiasts. They claim that these verses give them their warrant to tell every man, woman and child on this earth that Christ's salvation is for them.

---

[21] 2 Peter 1:20, 21.

71

The Free Offer

Ho, every one that thirsteth

Isaiah 55:1 ff., 'Ho, every one that thirsteth, come ye to the waters, and he that hath no money; come ye, buy and eat; yea, come, buy wine and milk without money and without price.' Fuller gives his basic exegesis of this text both in his *Christianity a Source of Happiness* and *The Gospel Worthy of All Acceptation* in which he argues that every man desires a good which has no limits and this verse appeals to this basic desire in man. Thus, so Fuller, Christ utilises this verse in drawing the sinner to Himself. The obvious retort is that if this were so, Christ would appeal to man's selfishness in order to save him. This does not worry Fuller at all as he believes that such a desire can be satisfied in Christianity rather than in other philosophies. Of fallen man, he says, 'Every one who looks into his own heart, and makes proper observations on the dispositions of others, will perceive that man is possessed of a desire after something which is not to be found under the sun—after a good which has no limits.[22] Echoing what he says in his work on holiness and happiness in *The Gospel Worthy of All Acceptation,* Fuller claims that the gospel call as illustrated by Isaiah 55 meets all that fallen man needs. Fuller thus concludes that here we have a gospel-offer. Indeed, for him, there can be no second opinion about the meaning of the text as The whole passage is exceedingly explicit, as to the duty of the unconverted; neither is it

---

[22] Christianity a Source of Happiness, *Works,* vol. II, p. 52.

possible to evade the force of it by any just or fair method of interpretation.'[23] The teaching is clear. It is the duty of the preacher to titillate the natural desires of man and tempt him to God by proclaiming that Christ can satisfy them. Any orthodox Christian must be baffled and shocked by such a gospel but we must not forget that Fuller is writing in all earnest and truly believes that what man takes up as a known duty, he will be able to perform and, in doing so, learn more about Christ. Indeed, it is Fuller's teaching that the more sinners practise keeping the law, the more they will learn to love Christ. Yet here, it would seem, according to Fuller, that we are not talking about keeping laws but merely following natural fallen instincts. This would be a wrong deduction. The natural longing for happiness which Fuller feels is in every man's heart, he believes, is the natural law of the nature and fitness of things, a law which also governs God's actions. Thus Fuller can argue that, The thirst which they are supposed to possess does not mean a holy desire after spiritual blessings, but the natural desire of happiness which God has implanted in every bosom, and which, in wicked men, is directed not to the sure mercies of David, but to that which is 'not bread' or which has 'no solid satisfaction in it'. This exposition would make the passage meaningless as a gospel encouragement as, according to Fuller, a spiritual response is not required but merely a 'natural' response.

---

[23] *Works*, vol. II, p. 344.

The Free Offer

Contrary to Fuller's view, however, the whole context of Isaiah 55 has to do with the spiritual relationship between Christ and His people—a relationship of grace.

What belongs to grace and the gospel in the passage is allotted to natural abilities, duties and the law by Fuller who after arguing that the thirsty ones are not initially spiritually motivated goes on to argue that when *thirst* is satisfied *duty* takes over, claiming then that, The duty to a compliance with which they are so pathetically urged, is a relinquishment of every false way, and a returning to God in His name who was given for "a witness, a leader, and a commander to the people" which is the same thing as "repentance towards God, and faith towards our Lord Jesus Christ."[24] Fuller can argue in this way as he believes that man has natural abilities to interpret natural revelation as pointing to spiritual things.

A text for chosen ones

Such a hypothesis can only be based on Isaiah 55 after taking the passage completely out of its Biblical context and placing it in Fuller's duty-faith environment. Whatever Fuller's views, however, it is obvious from the context that the text has to do with Christ and the people He chooses and not the masses seeking 'a natural desire of happiness'. It is refreshing to return to the true context of these evangelistic verses which are perhaps nowhere better

---

[24] Ibid, p. 344.

expounded than in the works of Particular Baptist John Gill. He must be given a say in this matter as those preachers of today who strive to appeal to sinners in Fullerite terms, denounce John Gill as if he had a different gospel—which of course he had, but one, as will be plain, that was planted, watered and reared in the pure ground of Scripture. Gill says of Isaiah 55:1-7:

> These words are no call, invitation, or offer of grace to dead sinners, since they are spoken to such who were *thirsty,* that is, who, in a spiritual sense, were thirsting after pardon of sin, a justifying righteousness, and salvation by Christ; after a greater knowledge of him, communion with him, conformity to him, and enjoyment of him in his ordinances, which supposes them to be spiritually alive; for such who are dead in sin, thirst not after the grace of God, but the lusts of the flesh, they mind and savour the things of the flesh, and not the things of the Spirit; only new-born babes, or such who are born again, are quickened and made alive, desire Christ, his grace, and the sincere milk of the word, that their souls may grow thereby; besides, the persons called unto, are represented as having no money; which, though true of unconverted persons, who have

nothing to pay off their debts, or purchase any thing for themselves; yet they fancy themselves to be rich, and increased in goods, and stand in need of nothing; whereas the persons here encouraged are such, who not only have no money, but know they have none; who are poor in spirit, and sensible of their spiritual poverty; which sense arises from the quickening influences of the Spirit of God upon their souls, nor are Isaiah 1:18, 19, Luke 13:3, John 3:16, and 8:24, any offers of grace, as they are with this represented to be.

No natural ability to approach God is addressed in the text

Gill continues by arguing that no power or natural ability to come to Christ in fallen man is presumed in the text nor any self-sufficiency in man to procure anything of himself by good works. The clear teaching of the text is thus that those come to God by means of being drawn to God by His specific and particular saving will. This is scandalous for modern Fullerites who will not believe that God speaks and draws individuals but that He merely provides a salvation for man in the bulk who can apply it to himself if he so wishes. For them, the duty of the preacher is done when he has presented the gospel. Now it is up to the hearers. In a mock conversation where Erroll Hulse in his work *The Free* Offer gives a 'modern example' (his own?) of a preacher speaking to one of his hearers, he has the hearer exclaim, 'You said just now that regeneration belongs to God. Now you tell me I must change my own heart!' To which the preacher replies, 'Yes! Absolutely! You are to change your own heart! By that I mean that the full weight of responsibility for what you are by nature as a sin-lover rests upon you. You are responsible to change your own heart. You are to do works meet for repentance. This means you are to make full use of the means God has provided for you.'[25] No pope could have put this better! The difference between Hulse and Gill whom the former appears to abhor and says quite untrue and unjust things about him in this work, is that whereas Hulse looks to man's responsibilities to make salvation perfect, Gill sees that those responsibilities merely condemn mankind and that the gospel to be preached to all men affirms that full salvation is of the Lord and anyone believing that they can team up with Christ in the business of salvation is like a man hoping that his own shadow will pull him out of a pit. Salvation is all of God or it is nothing.

As Isaiah 55 is used time and time again for free offer purposes, it is most important that the passage be studied in its right context as Gill does. When examined in this way, the passage can only be understood as God's providing of

---

[25] *The Free Offer*, p. 19.

salvation for a specific people whom He has chosen for that purpose. The preceding chapter shows how God is speaking of Christ's Bride, the elect, and not of the world in general, when he says 'For thy Maker is thine husband; the Lord of hosts is his name: and thy Redeemer the Holy One of Israel; The God of the whole earth shall he be called' (54:5). This Bride is promised everlasting kindness and mercy (v. 8) from the hand of the Lord which will never fail, 'For as I have sworn that the waters of Noah should no more go over the earth; so have I sworn that I would not be wrath with thee, nor rebuke thee. For the mountains shall depart, and the hills be removed; but my kindness shall not depart from thee, neither shall the covenant of my peace be removed, saith the Lord that hath mercy on thee' (v. 9, 10). As if not to allow any doubt on the matter, the Prophet stresses that, This is the heritage of the servants of the Lord, and their righteousness is of me, saith the Lord' (v. 17).

Not one Divine grace but two graces
Erroll Hulse ties himself in knots in his booklet *The Free Offer: An exposition of common grace and the free invitation of the Gospel.* Here, he not only speculates on a postulated two wills in God and a plurality of gospels in the Fuller-Murray tradition, but he also stipulates two kinds of grace on God's part, according to the two wills, here relying falsely on Abraham Kuyper, whom Hulse has most

certainly misunderstood.[26] As Hulse found one of the major works he consulted 'far from clear and badly translated',[27] he thus guards himself against misusing Kuyper, but perhaps should not have been so dogmatic in matters he finds unclear. Hulse thus affirms that there is a common grace which is given to all men and effectual grace which is given to the elect. However, just as Hulse's lip-service to election and predestination falls aside as a basis for the gospel of salvation and leaves him with a message of salvation to all, so his view of effectual grace falls aside in Hulse's enthusiasm for the balm-bringing effects of common grace as seen in the free offer. After spending pages doing away with the difference between his effectual and common graces, on page 7, Hulse can affirm that common grace carries with it the highest good God has for men and 'That God should thus address every creature with a saving Gospel is gracious and it is here that we see the connection between common grace and the free offer of the Gospel.' He then tells us that 'common grace finds its fullest expression in the provision of a Gospel to be addressed to all without exception.' Indeed, on page 8, Hulse goes on to say, 'Common grace, then, finds its highest expression in that desire and will of God not only for fallen man's temporal well-being but for his soul's

---

[26] David Engelsma deals with Hulse's misunderstanding and misapplication of Kuyper in his *Hyper-Calvinism and the Call of the Gospel,* Chapter 8, Kuyper's Doctrine of Particular Grace.
[27] *The Free Offer,* p. 21.

The Free Offer

salvation and eternal happiness.' Thus, though Kuyper spoke of common grace as the benevolence of God which causes the sun to shine on the just and unjust, and Hulse professes to lean on Kuyper's doctrine of general benevolence, he makes of it a dogma against which Kuyper was most opposed.

This is the work of God, that ye believe

John 6:29, 'This is the work of God, that ye believe on him whom he hath sent' has often been thrown at the author by zealous free offer men to 'prove' that God demands a work of duty-faith from those whom He will then accept. I never thought that I would live to be scolded by my fellow doctrines of grace men for claiming that this text shows clearly that God is the author of faith. One zealous defender of Fullerism, Robert Oliver, saw this statement of faith on my part as 'pouring scorn' on his master and, purporting to hide behind Calvin himself, he argued that this passage does not teach that faith is the gift of God but it is about what is required of man.[28] My argument was simply that Fuller had completely misunderstood the text, claiming that Christ was appealing to the Jews to practise Duty-Faith. Indeed, Fuller says of this text This is the first and greatest of all duties, and without it no other duty can be accept-

---

[28] *Banner of Truth Magazine,* Issue 376, Jan. 1995, pp. 11. The magazine would not allow me to defend my position regarding Robert Oliver's attacks but *Focus* printed my retort as *Robert Oliver and the Twists and Turns of Historical Revisionism, Focus,* No. 14, Summer, 1995, pp. 8-11.

able.'[29] William Button the Particular Baptist publisher told Fuller that he could not be serious believing that, but Fuller replied, 'From the connexion of this passage it was observed that the phrase *work of God* could not be understood of a work which God should work in them, but of a work which he *required* of them.'[30] However, the passage shows clearly that what God requires of man, He alone can give.

The context of Fuller's application of John 6:29 is in *The Gospel Worthy of All Acceptation* where he is talking of those in Isaiah 55:1-7 who hunger and thirst after righteousness and pardon. Fuller rejects any spiritual interpretation of this passage and then goes on to say that 'the New Testament is still more explicit than the Old' and quotes John 6:29 to underline what man in his fallen nature is expected to do, namely, respond to his natural duties, i.e. abilities. Let us look closely at John 6:29 which cannot possibly carry Fuller's meaning.

In verse 27 Jesus is teaching that the believer's labour is determined by God who marks him out and seals him for that purpose. Next Christ's general hearers ask Him what is to be done so that they might be sealed and be given everlasting food. 'You must believe in me', Christ tells them (v. 29). Now Christ's hearers do not ask Him how they can work to obtain this belief but how Jesus will work

---

[29] Gospel Worthy of All Acceptation, *Works*, vol. II, pp. 345, 346.
[30] Ibid, Reply to Mr Button, p. 429.

to give them that belief (v. 30). They even remind Jesus that their believing fathers had found life in God's works, without their own works. They were given bread from heaven (v. 31).

Jesus then goes on to say that such an earthly miracle has its parallels in heavenly ones. The heavenly bread of God is none other than Christ Himself who gives that life which brings eternal salvation with it (vs. 33-35). Then {v. 37) Christ graciously and with heavenly authority, says, 'All that the Father giveth me shall come to me; and him that cometh to me I will in no wise cast out.'

Oliver, in his criticism of my position, is obviously frightened that such an interpretation takes man's responsibility too lightly, so he sides with Fuller who lays the onus of activity on man. This is not Christian logic. No true Christian would deny that man is responsible for not believing but he would, I trust, deny that man has any natural abilities to exercise faith. When Fuller says, 'men have the same power, strictly speaking, before they are wrought upon by the Holy Spirit, as after; and before conversion as after; that the work of the Spirit endows us with no new rational powers, nor any powers that are necessary to moral agency;' he is both implying that fallen man has still the natural ability to believe and also denying the total depravity of man whose sin 'marred all' and even drew nature itself down with his total fall. Nevertheless Oliver challenges my statement that Fuller taught that God would never demand of man what he could not naturally do. A brief glance through his *The Gospel Worthy of All Acceptation* will show that Fuller majors on this very point. Arthur Kirkby is quite correct when he so succinctly sums up Fuller's belief in the words 'I could if I would'.[31]

A major flaw

Obviously the main weakness of the free offer dogma is that in warranting and offering salvation to all, sinners are being offered the gospel who have no ability of their own to accept it. Here Fullerites disagree. In a letter to Dr John Ryland, Fuller, the self-styled Strict Calvinist claims, 'If there were not sufficiency in the atonement for the salvation of sinners, and yet they were invited to be reconciled to God, they must be invited to what is *naturally impossible*.[32] The message of the gospel would in this case be as if servants who went forth to bid the guests had said "Come," though, in fact, nothing was ready if many of them had come.'[33] What Fuller is actually saying is that fallen man is naturally able to appropriate the gospel savingly. Here, Fuller is correct in his initial logic, but illogical in his deductions from it. Salvation is impossible

---

[31] See Arthur Kirkby, *The Theology of Andrew Fuller and its relation to Calvinism,* Ph.D., Edin., 1956, p. 160.
[32] Fuller's emphasis.
[33] *Works,* vol. II, p. 709.

for man but with God all things are possible, especially salvation.

No natural impossibilities

In his *The Gospel Worthy of all Acceptation,* Fuller points out that man is aware by the exercise of his natural abilities and his contact with the law that he has a natural duty to exercise faith savingly and, indeed, a natural ability to do so. This faith is directed to Christ who demands it of every man as his duty. Fuller can thus say, 'If faith in Christ be the duty of the ungodly, it must of course follow that every sinner, whatever his character, is completely warranted to trust in the Lord Jesus Christ for the salvation of his soul.'[34]

This doctrine of Fuller's is highly rationalistic and Pharisaic in origin. It virtually teaches that nature points the way, not only to a Creator but to a Saviour. Furthermore, it claims that following the Moral Law introduces the one prepared to do his duty savingly to Christ. Fuller assures the sinner that he has the natural abilities to follow this course, should he but be willing to use them.[35] 'No natural impossibilities' regarding man's salvation became a slogan with Fuller.[36]

---

[34] Ibid, Concluding Reflections, p. 383

[35] See Every man is bound cordially to receive and approve whatever God reveals, *Works,* vol. II, pp. 347-352; Whether Faith is required by the Moral Law, vol. II, p. 483; On Faith being a Requirement of the Moral Law, vol. II, p. 539 ff.

[36] See *Works,* vol. II, p. 345, 374.

Here we are back to the Moral Suasion of the Deists and Anglican Latitudinarians. Theirs was the gospel of the Rational Proposal of Duty which would enable a man to turn from sin to Christ and become a duty-bound Christian. We thus find Archbishop Tillotson (1630-1698) speaking of the natural duties of man in a sermon entitled *The Wisdom of Being Religious,* and arguing that the knowledge of duty is the image of God in man. Of this awareness of duty, he says:

For to know our duty, is to know what it is to be like God in *goodness,* and *pity,* and *patience,* and *clemency,* in *pardoning injuries,* and *passing by provocations',* in *justice and righteousness,* in *truth* and *faithfulness,*[37] and in hatred and detestation of the contrary of these: In a word, it is to know what is the good and acceptable will of God, what it is that he loves and delights in, and is pleased withal, and would have us to do in order to our perfection and our happiness.[38]

Tillotson defined 'religion' as a coming to God through obeying one's duty. Whether one 'came' or not indicated whether one was dutiful or not. Tillotson argued in this way because he believed that one could find the full gospel in the law and if one obeyed the law, one automatically obeyed the gospel. Here Tillotson has lost sight of the fall and the need for justification through faith which is a gift of

---

[37] Tillotson's emphasis.
[38] *The Works of the Most Reverend Dr John Tillotson,* London, 1704, p. 5.

The Free Offer

God who approaches man by Grace. He sees duty-faith rather as a matter of natural religion and within the scope of man's natural powers.

False duties lead to false faith

This belief is as false a view of duty as it is of faith and is thus not a gospel worth being offered freely. Those who have been introduced to the law certainly have a duty to keep it. Needless to say, one can only have a duty towards the law when the law is given. Paul says in Romans 7:7, 8: 'I had not known sin, but by the law: for I had not known lust, except the law had said, Thou shalt not covet ... For without the law sin was dead.' Similarly, one can only have a duty to faith when faith is given. When faith comes, one has no faith in one's own ability to exercise faith savingly. One's duty is then first and foremost not to the law, nor to faith itself, but to Christ who is the End of the Law and the Giver of faith and the only One able to save.

Preaching repentance and faith

Scripture teaches man's duty to repent. Scripture also teaches that man has no natural abilities to do so. He is dead in trespasses and sins. If he could repent, there would be life in him. The New Testament method of preaching is to turn the conscience of the sinner to the law he has broken and preach the need for repentance and the need for faith in the Saviour who has kept the law for him. Thus, in

Scripture all sinners are called to repentance (Mark 2:17; Luke 5:32 etc.). Hence repentance must be preached to all nations (Luke 24:47). Now the point is, are sinners to be *offered* repentance, are they to be *invited* to repent, or do we as God's ambassadors *command and call* people to repent? Scripture nowhere refers to offering repentance though we read of God *granting* repentance (Acts 5:31; 11:18; 2 Timothy 2:25). We also read of God *leading* sinners to repentance (Romans 2:4). The Christian's calling and duty in evangelisation is to follow Christ's example and *call* and *command* sinners to repentance (Matthew 9:13; Luke 5:32; Acts 17:30).

Where is the sinner called upon to exercise duty in keeping the Law? Ecclesiastes 12:13 says 'Fear God and keep his commandments for this is the whole duty of man.' This is also implied in Luke 17:10. where we read, 'So likewise ye, when ye shall have done all those things which are commanded of you, say we are unprofitable servants: we have done that which was our duty to do.'

The question now is, how does the sinner know he ought to repent? Does it come from an inner recognition of duty? Through an innate knowledge of responsibilities? Through a reason which is just as sharp after the Fall as before? No. Scripture makes it clear that fallen man is not aware of any such duties or responsibilities, nor has he any 'natural abilities' to live a perfect, law-conforming life.[39] He does

---

[39] 1 Corinthians 2:14 ff; Romans 1-3.

not know Christ to repent and exercise duty-faith in Him. If fallen men had known Christ, whom to know is life eternal, they would not have crucified the Lord of Glory.[40]

Law duties and faith confused

We notice then that the command to exercise duty applies to the law but it is used by Fullerites to mean a duty to exercise saving faith in Christ which belongs to Grace. How then does a sinner repent, or more Biblically put, how do the elect repent so that they may receive the remission of sins and faith in Christ? Not by having their sense of duty appealed to. This would be merely appealing to their pride. Repentance is plainly and simply given by God (Acts 5:31). God grants repentance (Acts 11:18). God's goodness leads to repentance (Romans 2:4). God does all this by working in man a godly sorrow for his sins (2 Corinthians 7:10). Is this gift of repentance conditional on man's display of duty-faith or is it discriminating according to God's will? It is surely discriminating as 2 Timothy 2:25 shows, 'If God *peradventure* will give them repentance.' The word υηποτε here surely means it is up to God's will.

But now the Fullerites will say, 'It is all very well you talking about duty to the law, but we talk about the duty of

---

sinners in respect of saving faith. Sinners are no longer under a law which is life, if obeyed.'[41]

Here Fullerites are denying the work of the law which demonstrates God's eternal standards, reveals man's sin, and pronounces him unsavable if left to himself. The law is shown to man as a life-earning pattern which he cannot possibly keep. The promises point to a Messiah to come who will keep it for us. Until Christ comes into the life of the sinner, he is still under the law which is life //obeyed and still under the penalty of death because he disobeys it. The law thus cannot give man life but death. Only dead men, according to the Scriptures can be made alive again, born again. Free offer people ignore this and invite sinners to exercise saving faith before the law has been allowed to do its work. They wish to revive men before they are diagnosed as dead. In emphasising man's abilities and natural powers, they brush aside man's total inability and powerlessness to comprehend both his own state and the gospel—however modified.

---

[41] *Works,* vol. II, p. 375, 376. See especially, 'God requires nothing of fallen creatures as a term of life. He requires them to love him with all their hearts, the same as if they had never apostasized.'

The Free Offer

go *Topical*

Part Four

Rightly Dividing The Word Of Truth

No general warrant of grace

The big question now is, does the Bible invite all men indiscriminately and everywhere to believe as Fuller maintains? No, says the Bible. Repentance must come first. Belief is always dependent on repentance. Repent ye and believe the gospel (Mark 1:15). When God grants repentance we may talk of belief but not before.

Where does this belief come from? Is it for all to grasp at, spurred by a knowledge of their duties? No. Belief

91

comes solely through God's sovereign will: 'I have chosen you that you might know and believe me and understand...' (Isaiah 43:10). Belief comes through Christ (John 1:17) and is the work of God (John 6:29). The non-elect may have this gospel declared to them—but only to their confounding: 'A work which ye shall in no wise believe, though I declare it unto you' (Acts 13:41). Only those who are chosen can know and understand what faith in Christ is. This is made obvious in 2 Thessalonians 2:13 where we read 'God hath from the beginning chosen you to salvation through sanctification of the Spirit and belief of the truth.'

Sinners cannot possibly have any inkling of responsibilities towards saving faith as God has withheld these truths from them as fallen creatures. Their natural, fallen abilities are of no help whatsoever. When they are granted repentance, faith, justification and sanctification—then they know how to live the Christian life.

Thus the command to exercise duty-faith can only be given to those who have a faith to exercise dutifully and a knowledge of their duties towards God. But faith is God's gift to His elect. It is not offered and then given when God sees that the sinner is ready to accept it. It is given with the same divine authority that God uses when He grants repentance. It is this gift of faith and this alone that justifies and thus distinguishes between believers and unbelievers. In preaching or not preaching duty-faith, the duty to exercise faith savingly, the difference between orthodox preachers such as John Gill and unorthodox such as Andrew Fuller becomes evident. Fuller preaches to believers only, Bible preachers preach to win lost sinners for Christ.

Graham Harrison in his booklet *John Gill and His Teaching,* censures Gill on the issue of duty-faith arguing that 'Gill and his friends laboured under the philosophical delusion that if faith is a gift, it cannot be a duty.' Here the confusion lies with Harrison. Gill was quite clear in his mind that the Christian had a duty to the God who had granted him faith and few spoke so much of the duties of the faithful as Gill. In his sermon on 'The Just Ruler found in Christ', Gill lists the duties of a Christian in respect to Christ as a ruler of men, and the church as the people of God and his obligation to work hard for the enlargement of Christ's Kingdom.[42] This is all in keeping with Gill's Biblical duty-faith teaching that with the grant of faith comes the obligation to exercise it. What Gill could not believe was that the duty of the evangelist was to preach that sinners were duty bound to exercise a faith savingly of which they knew nothing and of which they had nothing.

Thus, to orthodox men, faith is not of ourselves, it is a gift of God (Ephesians 2:8). Fuller, however says: The gospel is a feast freely provided, and sinners of mankind are freely invited to partake of it. There is no mention of a gift, or grant, distinct from this, but this itself is a ground

---

[42] *Sermons & Tracts,* Vol. II, p.47.

sufficient.'[43] Here we see that strange mixture of Bible knowledge and rationalism which is so much part and parcel of the free offer system. Fuller is not denying that faith is a gift but he is asserting that this gift is given only where it is offered and accepted by the action of the sinner exercising his natural moral duty. It is as if every man is born with a natural understanding of how things should be. The onus of acceptance lies with man rather than the initiative in giving coming from God. In his effort to emphasise man's ability to react responsibly, Fuller is ignoring God's sovereignty in having mercy on whom He will have mercy. Fuller is also attributing abilities to man which he lost at the Fall.

The right and wrong use of free offer terminology
Formerly, the term 'offer' either meant Christ's sacrifice on the cross or the presenting of the gospel as used in the *Westminster Confession* and the *Canons of Dort.* These Christian standards ruled out any application of the word in the meaning given it by Fuller, Murray and Hulse. However, in the 18th century Alvery Jackson, followed by Robert Hall Sen. and Andrew Fuller redeveloped the term to include the very universalism which the original uses denied it contained. This is why great evangelists such as Richard Davis and John Gill decided to drop using the term as it had become misleading.

---

[43] *Works,* Vol. II, p. 338. See pp. 335-338.

Fuller measures himself against Walter Marshall on the
offer, comparing himself with a giant. Marshall's *Gospel
Mystery of Sanctification,* one of the classics of Christian
doctrine, explains the full gospel of salvation in minute
detail to the praise of God. Marshall uses 'offer'
terminology as freely as Fuller, yet he uses it in quite
another context. The offer to Marshall is the conferring of
the right and duty to receive Christ's salvation as one's
very own. With this right and duty comes the gift of salvation itself.[44] This gift of salvation, joining the sinner to
Christ in a mystical union, is to be found fully in the
sovereign active will of God in which the object of
salvation is initially passive. Marshall says:

Thus we are passive, and then active, in this great work
of mystical union; we are first apprehended of Christ, and
then we apprehend Christ. Christ entered first into the soul,
to join Himself to it, by giving it the spirit of faith; and so
the soul receives Christ and His Spirit by their own power;
as the sun first enlightens our eyes and then we can see it
by its own light. We may further note, to the glory of the
grace of God, that this union is fully accomplished by
Christ giving the spirit of faith to us even before we act that
faith in the reception of Him; because, by this grace or
spirit of faith, the soul is inclined and disposed to an active
receiving of Christ.[45]

[44] *Gospel Mystery of Sanctification,* Evangelical Press, 1981, p. 52.
[45] Ibid, pp. 57, 58.

The Free Offer

Marshall never detracts in his use of the term 'offer' from its sacrificial meaning of Christ offering Himself for His Church. If this usage were universally followed, there would be no misunderstanding concerning the term and thus no harm done in using it but rather much good. Marshall's use of the term in relation to Christ's gift of Himself in giving His imputed righteousness to His elect, is regarded by many free offer men as being 'Hyper-Calvinist' as it emphasises God's sovereignty over man's responsibility. In so doing, however, they make nonsense of the term 'Hyper-Calvinism' and turn their backs on the Bible doctrine of the gospel mystery of sanctification.

The Marrow Men

Thomas Boston in his meticulous notes on *The Marrow of Modern Divinity* obviously believes in the offer of the gospel and interprets Edward Fisher's emphasis on preaching the gospel to all in this way. He, however, sees the authentic gospel offer as being the 'deed of gift or grant' given by God the Father, 'moved by nothing but his free love to mankind'[46] to whosoever receives it. He leans in this interpretation on the findings of the Synod of Dort. This gospel must be broadcast to all but it is not a gospel of universal redemption, nor even of universal atonement but the divinely ordained means of reaching the elect for whom

---

[46] *The Marrow of Modern Divinity,* Edward Fisher, ed. Thomas Boston, Philadelphia, undated, p. 126 ff.

Christ died. When this deed of gift or grant comes to a sinner 'to whom it doth not belong particularly, that man hath no warrant to believe on Jesus Christ.' Pardon, however, which is preached to the elect is preached to them by God's messengers because it has already been granted. This is the point where Fuller is not in harmony with the Marrow Men. Fuller believes that pardon comes when faith is exercised. The Marrow Men believed that pardon comes to whom pardon has been granted. It is a gift emanating purely from the will of God who has decided before the foundation of the world who will be saved. Hulse, dazzled by the Marrow Men's use of the (to him) magic word 'offer' claims them as his allies.[47] However, Fuller makes it clear that the free offer view and that of the Marrow Men are direct opposites.[48]

James Hervey

If Fuller disagreed with the Marrow Men then it is not surprising that he disagreed with James Hervey[49] who preached the offer in the sense of the Marrow-Men a generation before Fuller re-introduced the duty-faith preaching of the Anglican Latitudinarians. Of *The Marrow of Modern Divinity* Hervey says:

---

[47] *The Free Offer,* p. 10.
[48] *Works,* vol. II, p. 335 ff.
[49] Ibid, p. 335.

The Free Offer

It is a most valuable book; the doctrines it contains are the life of my soul, and the joy of my heart. Might my tongue or pen be made instruments to recommend and illustrate, to support and propagate such precious truths, I should bless the day wherein I was born. Mr. Boston's Notes on the 'Marrow' are, in my opinion, some of the most judicious and valuable that ever were penned.[50]

In his sermon on Ezekiel 18:27 which he called 'The Way of Holiness' Hervey emphasises that:

The Holy Ghost, in all his operations, and with all his graces, Christ sends to whomsoever he pleases. He gave this inestimable blessing to Saul the persecutor and blasphemer: he gave this inestimable blessing to many of his murderers and crucifiers: he still confers the heavenly gift on his enemies; *yea, on the rebellious also.* And the promise, the free gracious promise, *is to you, and to your children, and to all that are afar off, even as many as the Lord our God, by the preaching of his gospel, shall call.*

---

[50] Extract from a letter to William Hogg.

Hervey did not mention Saul, Christ's crucifiers and other rebels without due thought. He did so to emphasise that God grants salvation without any preparatory steps on the part of those to whom salvation is granted. It is while we are rebels that the gift comes to us. It was in the very moment that Saul was breathing out fire and slaughter against the will of God that he experienced God's converting will in his own life.

William Huntington

It will come as a big, big, surprise to modern free offer men to find that William Huntington spoke, like the Marrow Men, of an 'offer' in the gospel, though, like them, he did not put a 'free' in front of the term. Huntington never ceased to speak of the gospel offer. Also, like the Marrow Men, Huntington spoke of the gospel offer of Christ within His covenant. When preaching, he would use such words as 'Those that are weary and heavy laden are called; the lame, the halt, and maimed, are invited ... all that hunger and thirst are welcome; and those made willing to close with the gospel offer, and hold the truth as it is in Christ, have a right by divine invitation.'[51] Writing of a lady who had just died in the full assurance of faith, he wrote 'She closed in with the offer, and made a match with the heavenly Bridegroom, while I was publishing the bans.'[52] Speaking

[51] *Works,* vol. VI, Epistles of Faith, p. 107.
[52] Ibid, p. 370.

The Free Offer

of the worldwide application of the gospel, Huntington could affirm in the *Arminian Skeleton,* 'Out of each host the elect of God will one day be called; and a light sufficient will be given them to discover the enemies of their liberties, to which, by a covenant of sovereign grace, they were predestinated.'

The Free Offer, no shibboleth for orthodoxy

On examining what preachers of the past have understood by the 'offer', it becomes obvious that the term is little use as a means of distinguishing extremists from the orthodox as those who stress God's side in salvation and those who stress human responsibility and those who stress both have all used the term. It is also used by those who would deliberately shut out much of the gospel from their preaching, feeling that it is unsuitable for unconverted ears. There are sadly modern free offer preachers who follow Fuller in claiming that the full gospel, including predestination and election is for believers only and thus not to be placed in the 'free offer'. Nowadays, all who use the term the 'free offer' appear to limit its contents. If we could define the 'free offer' as indicating Christ's call to take the gospel to all the world, it would be a meaningful, usable term, though not a Biblical one. Similarly, if we could define the words 'free offer' as referring to Christ's substitutionary and redemptive death on the cross alone, we would have a basis for using the word which is descriptive

100

of the gospel and has the advantage of being a Biblical term. This would, of course, still present difficulties for those, as Fuller, who believe that the atonement did not virtually and vicariously redeem anyone but merely made redemption possible. In the opinion of this author, however, such people do not perform the work of a gospel evangelist and their opinions and definitions of the 'free offer' are thus of little importance. This is one big reason why the term ought to be dropped, especially as it is not a Biblical term such as justification, redemption etc.. It would be helpful if the term duty-faith were dropped for the same reasons. Then people could get on with their call to preach without fearing that their brethren in Christ will strive to thwart their endeavours by claiming that they ought to use shibboleths. This is indeed the naive, misguided view of one writer in the so-called Moderate Calvinist section who believes that the use or non-use of the term 'offer' in its universal sense separates the Calvinists from the Hyper-Calvinists.[53]

The full gospel versus the Free Offer
Gill's *Declaration of Faith* is a faithful testimony to the gospel which Gill taught and a sure guide to readers as to the scope and effect of the gospel to be preached to all as the Spirit leads. In that statement and Gill's comments on it one word occurs frequently: the word 'duty'. Here is meant

---

[53] See Curt Daniel's *Hyper-Calvinism and John Gill*.

however, not Christian duties expected of non-Christians as in the duty-faith teaching but the duties of Christians to take the whole gospel to all mankind. Of Gill's summary of what he believed and preached in his 1729 *Declaration,* John Rippon says:

> This form of sound words, containing the substance of his early creed, he maintained, without deviation, to the very end of his days; and few are the formulas which have at any time been more closely united with *duty.* The term and the thing are remarkable, in this confession—and no man was more fond of either in their proper place, and fairly understood.[54]

Repentance and faith

In expounding 2 Timothy 1:13 'Hold fast the form of sound words', Gill, following Paul, reduces the sum of the gospel under two heads, repentance towards God and faith towards our Lord Jesus Christ (Acts 20:21). He also accepted as a pattern for preaching Romans 8:29, 30 outlining the doctrine of effectual calling, predestination, justification

---

[54] *Life and Writings of the Rev. John Gill, DD,* John Rippon, Gano Books, 1992, p. 20.

and glorification. These are doctrines which many who use the words 'free offer' remove from their message to sinners, believing that they are for believers only. Cotton Mather, in criticising the duty-faith teaching of his day, outlines how this kind of preaching leaves out predestination and election which are two of the most comforting doctrines to sinners that the gospel affords. He put the weak effects of preachers in his own day down to a refusal to expound this gospel. As he himself was one of the most successful preachers and pastors America ever had, one cannot say that preaching election frightened the people from the churches.[55] Attempts have been made by such as Erroll Hulse in his Free Offer booklet to show that Gill was unsuccessful in drawing souls to Christ through preaching such 'Hyper-Calvinistic doctrines', but the statistics speak for themselves. Gill's church membership was for a long time the largest of any Baptist Church in Britain and Gill gathered large numbers in lecture halls. Whilst Fuller confessed at the end of his life that his church members had been decreasing for twenty-five years,[56] free-grace (rather than free offer) congregations were growing rapidly in Anglican, Independent and Baptist churches. Within a generation Fuller's Northampton association was

---

[55] See Cotton Mather's *Free Grace,* Boston, 1706.
[56] *Works,* vol. Ill, pp. 481-489. John Stevens' *Help for the True Disciples of Immanuel,* pp. v, vi, Kenneth Dix' *Particular Baptists and Strict Baptists, An Historical Survey,* pp. 4, 6, 7 and passim.

denying the inerrancy and infallibility of the Scriptures as also the Scriptural doctrine of holiness.

A true witness to the person of God and His eternal love for the elect

Keeping to the same text, Gill goes on to outline that within the pattern of sound words which was committed to Timothy to preach was the proper deity and unity of the Godhead. For Gill the modern evangelical doctrine that Christ had a different will to His Father concerning salvation would have been damned as the heresy it is.

Next Gill emphasises that part of the gospel is the eternal love of the Triune God to His elect and Christ's surety arrangements for them. He stresses the total depravity of man and his total inability and impotence to do anything spiritually good of himself. He includes particular redemption, satisfaction for sin by Christ's sacrifice, free and full pardon by His blood, justification by His imputed righteousness, regeneration and sanctification by the powerful and efficacious grace of the Spirit of God, the final perseverance of the saints to eternal glory as the free gift of God and much, much more.

Similar long lists of all that a preacher should teach are to be found in Gill's commentaries on Galatians 1:23, 2 Corinthians 1:19 and in his remarks on Proverbs 15, Acts 10, Mark 16 and a number of his other works. Few preachers have stressed as Gill what the full scope of the gospel is and the need to preach it. The gospel to Gill is the sum total of all that the Father, Son and Holy Spirit have done and do and reveal in the Word. Not a jot or tittle must be left out.

Christ Biblically presented

For Gill Christianity was Christ but he did not merely appeal to his hearers to accept Christ as if all knew inherently who Christ was. His gospel was not that Christ loved all so all must love Christ, and that is that! For Gill the gospel revealed Christ as 'really and proper God, and truly man; that he is the Son of God, and the Mediator between God and men; that he is the Messiah, who is actually come in the flesh; that he died and rose again the third day; is ascended into heaven, and sits at the right hand of God, and will come a second time to judge the world in righteousness; and that by his obedience and sufferings, and death, he has become the Saviour of sinners, and that none can be saved but by him.'[57]

Preaching the whole counsel of God

Many similar descriptions of the Christ who is to be preached to all men are to be found throughout Gill's works where he stresses time and time again the need to preach the whole counsel of God. In *The Watchman's Answer to*

---

[57] *The Cause of God and Truth*, p.31.

The Free Offer

the Question What of the Night, Gill deals with the general decay in church growth of his day (1750). The cause, he finds, lies chiefly in the work of gospel ministers who hold back vital doctrines in a vain effort to be 'popular' and appeal to all. He tells these preachers that:

> ... they should watch, and stand fast in the faith, and quit themselves like men, and be strong; and they should not conceal any thing that ought to be known, or keep back that which is profitable, but declare the whole counsel of God. Their work is to warn sinners of their evil ways, and of the danger they are in by them; to shew them what an evil and bitter thing sin is, and that the wrath of God is revealed from heaven against it; that the wages of sin is death eternal; and that destruction and mercy are in all their ways, in which they will issue, if grace prevent not; and to convince them of the worth of their precious and immortal souls, and that nothing can be given in exchange for them.[58]

This is preaching the gospel properly.

---

[58] *Sermons & Tracts* I, pp. 38, 39.

go *Topical*

Adding and subtracting

Free offer man Curt Daniel's response to Gill's repeated emphasis on the whole gospel shows what antagonism there is amongst modern would-be evangelists against preaching a full gospel.[59] He accuses Gill of *adding* superfluous tenets. He is actually fearful that Gill includes too much in his good news for sinners rather than too little! To labour his point, Daniel argues, without giving a scrap of evidence, that Gill refused to support Whitefield, thinking he subtracted from the gospel and, indeed, such as Whitefield actually opposed Gill. Such remarks concerning Whitefield and his circle are typical of the free offer lobby who pass on such idle gossip from publication to publication. Gill and Whitefield were both so intent on preaching the full gospel that they did not bother about the petty bickering which mars Daniel's work. If Daniel had done his homework, he would have found records of Gill visiting Whitefield at his Tabernacle House, Moorfields and sharing there the work of evangelism with such as his host, Romaine, Hervey, Gifford, Cudworth and Cennick. Does Daniel feel that Whitefield would have invited Gill to give a talk in his parlour on the duties of ministers if he opposed him? Lady Huntingdon and her band of ministers respected and honoured Gill greatly and, as Thomas Wright

---

[59] *John Gill and Hyper-Calvinism*, p. 395.

107

so aptly put, Carter Lane was Toplady's alma mater.[60] Gill was closely attached to the Whitefield circle meeting at the Countess Delitz', Lady Hotham's and Lady Shirley's, possibly through Hervey, and Whitefield was instrumental in supporting a number of Gill's fellow Baptist pastors.[61] Hervey is full of glowing anecdotes regarding his friends Gill, Brine, Ryland Sen. and Cudworth who obviously moved in his own circle which had Whitefield at the centre.

The Free Offer dogma is built on speculative metaphysics not Biblical theology

One of the main dangers of using the phrase 'free offer' is that its users invariably become embarrassed as to what they should include in the offer and to whom it should be free. This, just as invariably, leads them into metaphysical speculations in their eagerness to analyse the will of God concerning to whom and what is to be preached. This danger is nowhere more evident than in the writings of free offer enthusiasts who with greater or lesser surgical skills strive to dissect the mind of God into its desires and decrees; original intentions and subsequent intentions; revealed will and secret will; original design and modified design; special love and universal love; common grace and saving grace. Particularly the Fullerite dissecting of man

---

[60] *The Life & Times Of Selina, Countess of Huntingdon,* vol. I, p. 113. *Augustus Toplady,* p. 15.
[61] Ibid, vol. I, pp. 162, and passim.

into his supposedly non-fallen and fallen elements and his presumed natural and moral abilities is to be questioned.[62] It is not the work of an evangelist to speculate in this way. His business is to preach the whole gospel where he is sent and to whom he is sent. He does not bring the same message to all men as to some it comes as a message of death and damnation alone and to others it accomplishes a raising from the dead.

The gospel preached can be likened to the Apostles' fishing expedition in John 21. Without Jesus to guide them the would-be fishermen caught nothing. When they cast out their net in accordance with Christ's will, it was filled. The disciples did not know where the fish were or which fish they should catch. They did what they were told and they were successful. The Bible is full of advice as to how the gospel should be preached. Sinners must be called, commanded, even beseeched to repent and turn from their evil ways. God commands all to repent and grants repentance to some who would not otherwise repent. It is presumptuous to believe that we can offer, in God's name that repentance and that turning. This would be foolish thinking that we can take over God's initiative in salvation. It would be casting the net on the wrong side of the ship.

Perhaps, to preserve the bonds of peace, we should have no quarrel with those who use the term 'free offer' yet preach the full gospel, though they may be unwise to use

---

[62] Fuller's *Works*, vol. II, footnotes pp. 546, 547.

the term as it is ambiguous to the point of being quite misleading. It is another matter, however, with those who have broken the peace themselves and say that their brethren in Christ, who are often greater soul-winners, are nevertheless Antinomians and Hyper-Calvinists because they do not use the term 'free offer'. This erroneous position must be condemned. By their fruits God's servants are known and not by the way they coin phrases or stick to shibboleths. Anyone who studies the life and teaching of John Gill, the arch bogey-man of the free offer enthusiasts, will find that he remained as close as few have ever remained to the gospel pattern from his conversion to his death. It would be thus better to drop the phrase altogether than use it to condemn a great fisherman and to confuse the issue concerning where and when and for what fish the gospel net has to be cast out.

Part Five

The Free Offer: A Summary

The modern Free Offer is an approach to preaching designed to appeal to the natural man. It is thus a man-centred and philosophical approach to the gospel rather than a Christ-centred and Biblical approach. It credits the sinner with a natural ability to respond positively to the gospel message and undermines the eternal purpose of the Father in choosing, the atoning work of the Son in redeeming and the regenerating work of the Holy Spirit in calling, the elect.

The Free Offer

The Free Offer approach is to be rejected on the following grounds:

1. It has an insufficient view of the gospel which is not based on God's electing grace.
2. It has a faulty view of the atonement as merely a providing of salvation and not a procuring and securing of it.
3. It has a faulty view of God, a God who is at loggerheads with Himself.
4. It has a faulty view of man who is made an agent in salvation.
5. It is not an offer of full salvation as it leaves man to perform repentance and faith as conditions.
6. It is based on law-duties and not faith.
7. It teaches that law-duties beget faith.
8. It is a gospel to believers only, therefore it has no evangelistic purpose.
9. It does not pay due attention to the saving application of the gospel.
10. Nor does it pay attention to the fact that the gospel comes as a judge to some and a saviour to others.

Contrary to the above, we find in the Scriptures, exemplified by Ephesians Chapters 1 and 2, that:

1. Salvation starts and continues in heaven (1:3).

Paul, in Ephesians Chapter 1 tells us that God has decided for the very best of reasons who to save already in heaven, outside of time and irrespective of our personal wills, intentions and abilities. The blessings which anyone has in Christ are heavenly blessings, given him from heaven and not earned by him on earth.

2. Salvation is God's choice not man's (1:4).

God has chosen certain people from His vantage point in heaven to witness for Him on earth before they enter into an inheritance reserved for them eternally in heaven. He has, Scripture tells us in Ephesians 1:5, adopted those whom He has chosen 'according to the good pleasure of His will'. In other words, God had very good reasons for adopting certain sinners so that they might be re-created as children of God. These reasons are not entirely given us. We would most certainly not understand them. Nevertheless, Paul gives us some inkling in his first chapter of the epistle to Ephesus by saying that it was God's rich mercy, His great love, His wisdom, His prudence, His exceedingly rich grace and His kindness toward us that sealed our salvation. Such reasons ought to satisfy anyone!

3. God makes the unacceptable acceptable (1:6).

These sinners, the inspired writer tells us, are 'made acceptable'. They were, due to their own sinful state, highly unacceptable. Look at the state of sinners that God saves as revealed in Ephesians 2. They are 'dead in trespasses and sins', they are 'children of disobedience', they wallow in 'the lusts of the flesh', they are 'the children of wrath'. They are everything that must be unacceptable to a Holy God, yet that merciful, loving, kind and gracious God makes them acceptable. If He did not do it, *nobody* else could. Certainly we would never manage such a transformation ourselves.

How can a person dead in sin choose to make himself alive by suddenly accepting a guarantee of salvation? Scripture, and experience, teach us that the very idea of God is abhorrent to the sinner's nature. If he could choose the righteous God to aid him, he would not be dead in sin but be able to perform a righteous act. The Bible clearly teaches that There is none righteous, no, not one,' (Romans 3:1). Evidently, 'dead' means dead and not 'half alive'.

4. All those whom God elected to salvation will be saved (1:13)

Christ has redeemed His elect by His full and vicarious substitution on the cross (1:7). The blood of the Lord Jesus Christ has cleansed all for whom He died and not one of them is lost. The Free Offer is a gospel of absolute scepticism as it offers a salvation conditional on a response the sinner cannot possibly make.

5. All those who have been saved will be kept until they enter their eternal inheritance (1:14).

As Christ was raised up from the dead, those for whom He died will be likewise raised up to be with their Saviour for ever. This is the gospel worthy of acceptance.

May our final testimony as preachers of the full gospel be that of Paul as he looked back on his life as an evangelist before the martyr doors of the prison closed on him:

But none of these things move me, neither count I my life dear unto myself, so that I might finish my course with joy, and the ministry, which I have received of the Lord Jesus, to testify the gospel of the grace of God. And now, behold, I know that ye all, among whom I have gone preaching the kingdom of God, shall see my face no more. Wherefore I take you to record this day, that I am pure from the blood of all men. For I have not shunned to declare unto you all the counsel of God. Take heed therefore unto yourselves, and to all the flock, over which the Holy Ghost hath made you overseers, to feed the church of God, which he hath purchased with his blood. For I know this, that after my departing shall grievous wolves enter in among you, not sparing the flock. Also of your own selves shall men arise, speaking perverse things, to draw away disciples after them. Therefore watch and remember.

The Free Offer

go *Topical*

Indices

117

The Free Offer

Index Of Scripture Verses

Old Testament

The Free Offer

New Testament

Matthew
5:44-48	36
9:13	87
20:28	67
23:37	37
25:34	66

Mark
1:15	91
2:17	87
10:45	67
16	104

Luke
5:32	87
13:3	76
13:34	37
17:10	87
24:47	30, 31, 87

John
1:17	92
6:29	92
3:16	76
6:29	80, 81
8:24	76
17:3	88fn
17:23	66
21	109

Acts
5:31	87
11:18	87
14:17	37
17:30	87
20:28	69

Romans
1, 2	30
1-3	87fn
2:4	87, 88
3:1	114
5:9	69
7:7	86
7:8	86
8:29	102
8:30	102

1 Corinthians
1:23	10
1:24	10
2:8	88fn
2:14	87fn
6:20	51, 69
7:23	51, 69
15:55	66

2 Corinthians
1:19	104
7:10	88

Galatians
1:23	104
4:4	68

The Free Offer

Index of People

The Free Offer